SAFFRON
A COLLECTION OF PERSONAL NARRATIVES BY MUSLIM WOMEN

SAFFRON
A COLLECTION OF PERSONAL NARRATIVES BY MUSLIM WOMEN

Edited by
Dr Zaheera Jina

African Perspectives Publishing
PO Box 95342, Grant Park 2051, South Africa
www.africanperspectives.co.za

Publication © African Perspectives Publishing 2018
Text © Individual authors

All rights reserved.
No part of this publication may be reproduced,
stored in a retrieval system or transmitted in any form or by any means,
electronic, mechanical, photocopying or otherwise,
without the prior written permission of the editors.

ISBN PRINT 978-0-6399187-2-3
ISBN DIGITAL 978-0-6399187-3-0

Compiled and edited by **Dr Zaheera Jina**
Copyedited and proofread by **Liz Sparg**
Typeset by **Gail Day**
Cover design by **K Creative Design (Pty) Ltd**

Contents

	Introduction	ix
	LIVED REALITIES	1
1	Living as *awliya* – Safiyyah Surtee	2
2	Planning for the marriage vs planning for the wedding – Adela Bootha	9
3	The importance of a marriage contract – Papatia Feauxzar	13
4	Words of wisdom from my *Naani* – Safiyyah Sujee	18
5	An ideal world... – Mariam B. Daya	23
	Pearls of wisdom	29
	FOOD AND MARRIAGE	31
6	Ways to the heart: Food in our marriage – Saaleha Idrees Bamjee	32
7	Love, life and piping hot *roti* – Fatima Bheekoo-Shah	36
8	Toasted cheese sandwiches – Safeera Kaka	40
9	The taming of the shrew! – Hina Nafe	44

10 Food in a marriage – Afzad-Al _____ 48
11 Marriage is a feast – Nabihah Plaatjes _____ 51
12 Those first 30 cups of *roti* dough...
   – Maymoona Chohan _____ 57
13 Cooked! – Khalida Moosa _____ 61
14 *Khidmat* in the kitchen – Aneesa Bodiat-Sujee _____ 64
15 "Hungry, darling?" – Raashida Khan _____ 68
16 Some like it hot! – Gouwa Gabier _____ 73
17 The 'love story' kitchen – Quraisha Dawood _____ 77
18 If food be the music of love, play on...
   – Zayboon Motala _____ 81

   Pearls of wisdom _____ 85

   HARDSHIP AND CONFLICT _____ 86

19 My Bollywood movie love – Yumna Samaria _____ 87
20 From point A to point B; beyond ocean
   and continent – Najma Ansari _____ 93
21 Seek your husband's advice
   – Khairun-Nisaa Dadipatel _____ 97
22 At a time when marriage meant everything
   – Sabera Chothia _____ 99
23 Reflections of a daughter – Sumayya Mehtar _____ 103
24 Braving conflict and hardship with perseverance
   – Anonymous _____ 107
25 If only I had known – Nurnazida Nazri _____ 113
26 When 'the one' is the wrong one!
   – Shauqeen Mizaj _____ 116
27 Beautiful lies – Saffiya Ismail Cassim _____ 120

28 Understanding where conflicts come from
    – Anonymous _____ 127
29 When communication is not enough
    – Papatia Feauxzar _____ 130
30 Marriage and emotional disorders
    – Layla Abdullah-Poulos _____ 132
31 Surviving a traumatic incident: Lessons learnt
    – Shakira Akabor _____ 136

    *Pearls of wisdom*_____ 141

    DEALING WITH IN-LAWS _____ 143

32 A cup of milky white tea
    – Mumtaz Moosa Saley _____ 144
33 Your mother-in-law is not your enemy
    – Nabeela Noorani _____ 147
34 Dealing with in-laws – Zara Valli_____ 150
35 I married his family and they married me ...
    – Zaheera Jina _____ 153

    *Pearls of wisdom*_____ 159

    INTIMACY, BABY-MAKING AND CHILDREN _____ 161

36 My 'first night' – Afzad-Al _____ 162
37 Too painful to be pleasurable – Anonymous_____ 166
38 The etiquette to follow for the nuptial night
    – Papatia Feauxzar _____ 171
39 Sublime strawberries – N. Moola _____ 175
40 Life, lies and liberation – Quraisha Dawood _____ 179
41 Difficulties of conceiving – Anonymous _____ 184

42 Baby-making – Anonymous	188
43 When the body betrays – Dilshad Parker	192
44 My heart's story – Somayya Hansrod	196
45 Romance on pause – Ayesha Desai	203
46 Raising kids in the 21st century – Fatima Kazee	207
47 Porridge-brain syndrome – Feroza Arbee	210
48 When the father is a better parent – Razina Theba	214
Pearls of wisdom	218

THE SELF-ESTEEM OF A MUSLIM WOMAN — 220

49 Letter to my daughter – Rehana Moosajee	221
50 It's all about your mind-set… – Fatima Kazee	226
51 The fairest of us all – Yasmin Denat	230
52 Finding myself in my marriage – Maimoonah Gori	236
53 Writing my own script – Shaakira Rahiman-Saleh	240
54 Love lost and found – Waasila Jassat	247
55 Feeling beautiful in a marriage – Hawa Bibi Shahaboodien	255
56 "If you want to be original, be ready to be copied" – Jamela Garda	259
Pearls of wisdom	263
About the authors	265
Glossary	281

Introduction

It all started when I became an adult and developed an innate need to become a wife and mother. I had to wait almost a decade for this dream to be fulfilled; then, when eventually it did happen, I was naive in every sense of the word. There was so much that I didn't know, and not having sisters and older girl cousins made everything all the more daunting. I grew up with the advice to always be patient and to request guidance solely from my Creator. "Bedroom stories remain in the bedroom," they warned. When I got married, I received religious books as gifts, but their content did not assist with the reality of my experiences. I often felt frustrated and overwhelmed, but because I had been conditioned to believe in the notion of the religious sanctity of marriage, I remained silent.

My friend, Fatima, was always forthright with her advice. "Wake up ZJ!" she warned. "You are not getting any younger! Only a fertility specialist will be able to help!" Fatima unveiled my thoughts from the darkness that had been consuming me in my desperate obsession to have another baby. Our conversations got me thinking about societal and religious belief systems, the trials of intimacy and baby-making, and, of course, about Muslim women's self-esteem, which is often shattered through these experiences. It helped me immensely to hear Fatima's experiences and to share mine.

I had gathered anecdotal evidence about the difficulty of adjustment in marriages and living with in-laws, I had witnessed how friends and family members grew listless in their marriages over time, and I had experienced the extent to which divorce had shattered a close friend's self-esteem. Her *mahr* agreement was interpreted as prenuptial, thus preventing her from exercising her right to the marital estate and leaving her destitute after her divorce. She was forced to leave her husband's home, with her four young children, and live on the pittance that her husband paid for their maintenance. My friend's story is not unique. Her experiences remind me that our culture and religious beliefs do not always encourage pre-marital guidance and support, and led me to compile this collection.

The historical importance of marriage in Islam

In Islam it is generally believed that the Prophet Muhammad and the Quran significantly uplift the rights of women. Women enjoy separate but equally important roles in the institution of marriage, and each spouse owes a religious duty to the other: "They (your wives) are a clothing (covering) for you and you too are a clothing (covering) for them" (*Surah* 2, Verse 187). Marriage is central to Islam and is viewed as a safeguard of chastity and the key to social harmony. Marriage to a man is the culturally defined ultimate destiny for most Muslim women (Amer, Howarth and Sen, 2015). The significance of marriage in Islam is an approval of intercourse and the procreation of children between two equal partners, as well as the completion of human nature as created by Allah.

Before a marriage can take place, consideration of the social status of a potential spouse is required by the *Sharíah*, although it is not mandated by the Quran. The doctrine of equality requires that marriages should occur between men and woman of equal status, because, if marriages are to reinforce social harmony, society cannot afford to risk the instability inherent in unequal matches. The practical effect of this law is that a bride may only take a husband who is in an occupation either comparable or superior to the occupation of her father; however men may marry beneath them, raising the woman to their superior status through marriage. Similarly, women are prohibited from marrying non-Muslim men, while men are permitted to marry women from the Jewish and Christian faiths.

Once married, the husband's responsibility is to sustain his wife and family financially. Regardless of her own wealth, the wife is entitled to maintenance according to her husband's means, including food, clothing, housing, toiletries, medical attention, and helpers for those women in certain social positions. In theory – if not always in practice – a wife is not required to prepare food for her family, clean her home, or even nurse her baby, but if she chooses to do so, such acts are viewed as voluntary, charitable contributions, which she makes freely and willingly. Although Muslim women are routinely characterised as sexually oppressed, in the context of Islamic marriage women enjoy equal access to sex, which is viewed as neither sinful nor taboo.

Empirical research, however, shows that Muslim women often experience limited choice in marriage – a cultural rather than Islamic norm – and that a woman who exercises choice in marriage is perceived as a potential challenge to the institutions of family and community, even though it is acknowledged as a right given by Islam (Khurshid, 2014). In most countries, any attempt at feminist reform continues to be derided as immoral, heretical and a source of destruction to both the sanctity of the family and the basic pillars of Islam itself (Blenkhorn, 2002).

This collection: Personal narratives by Muslim women

While this anthology is situated in the context I have just described, it is not a research project and it does not make any specific points or arguments in relation to Muslim marriages. Instead, it aims, firstly, to capture a selection of Muslim women's experiences of marriage in their own words – words that will deeply touch and open your heart if you have ever been married, or hope to be married. Secondly, the anthology will contribute to a knowledge base containing the lived realities of Muslim women. Thirdly, these honest narratives may inform others in how they write and speak about Muslim women.

Sourcing the contributions to this anthology was a mammoth, yet rewarding, task. I was heartened when I read these personal narratives, and my prayer is that you will be, too. If you are not yet married, perhaps the stories will help you reflect on what marriage means, or, if you are married, to better understand your husband (and yourself), or help you appreciate your in-laws and see the good in what they do. The selection of stories in this anthology represents a wide range of Muslim women's experiences of marriage. They will remind and reassure you that, although marriage brings with it many challenges, you are never alone in what you go through – other women walk the journey with you.

I have arranged the stories in this collection in six sections. "Lived Realities" includes advice from Muslim women on the importance of the marriage contract and what to do prior to the wedding day. "Food and Marriage" features narratives describing how food is often central in bridging relationships. In "Hardship and Conflict", married women tell their stories and offer advice on challenges they have encountered. "Dealing with In-laws" features stories and advice from Muslim women who live or lived with their in-laws. "Intimacy, Baby-making and Children" includes advice on the nuptial night, how to keep the spark alive, the trials of conceiving offspring, and bringing up children. And the narratives in "The Self-esteem of a Muslim Woman" emphasise that women need to first love themselves unconditionally, before allowing anybody else to share in their lives.

Being a Muslim woman involves a perfect blend of saffron, rituals and philosophies. Only through descriptions of their lives are we allowed to walk with Muslim women, see what they see, and try to understand the complexity of their lives.

Dr Zaheera Jina

References

Amer, A., Howarth, C. and Sen, R. (2015) Diasporic virginities: Social representations of virginity and identity formation amongst British Arab Muslim women. *Culture and Psychology* 21(1):3-19.

Blenkhorn, L.E. (2002) Islamic marriage contracts in American courts: Interpreting *mahr* agreements as prenuptials and their effect on Muslim women. *Southern California Law Review* 76:189.

Khurshid, A. (2014) Islamic traditions of modernity: Gender, class, and Islam in a transnational women's education project. *Gender & Society* 29(1):98-121. DOI: https://doi.org/10.1177/0891243214549193.

LIVED REALITIES

As time went on, my husband and I realised that we had similar goals but we followed different paths to get there. Similar ideas, but different approaches. Similar needs, but different interests. My way always seemed best to me, and to him his way was better. While none of these differences were catastrophic, it still meant that nurturing the marriage required much hard work, patience, maturity and nerves of steel.

Adela Bootha

1

Living as *awliya*
Safiyyah Surtee

Two months before I turned twenty, I tied the knot in a huge, fairy-tale wedding, with a true Indian-style reception befitting the eldest child and only daughter of my parents. Over a decade later, I write this reflection on the growth and challenges a twelve-year relationship has brought.

Behind the fairy-tale wedding, there were many real-life considerations to take into account for a modern Muslim marriage. I wasn't involved in Muslim women's activism and advocacy back then. The year before I got married, I had just started studying towards a Bachelor of Arts, foraging in subjects like philosophy, anthropology, English literature and politics, and eventually majoring in Arabic and Islamic Studies. Many hours spent rummaging through the library shelves in the religion section introduced me to books about Islam and gender, and I began to read voraciously and think deeply, about marriage in Islam and Muslim cultures and about what it meant to be a gendered person. I learnt about age-old debates on the status of Muslim women, from family law, inheritance and testimony to dress code and sexuality. These issues resonated deeply with my experiences as a young woman in the patriarchal society I had grown up in – loving and benevolent, yes, but patriarchal, nonetheless, in terms of the expectations of women and the roles assigned to them.

Equipped with all this new (to me) information about the struggles of Muslim women all over the world, and the courage of scholars and activists who documented all this work, I decided to make sure my marriage started on a different footing. I wanted to create a foundation of equality and mutuality at the outset. Based on my year of reading and research , my husband and I decided to draw up a *nikah* contract – a mechanism that is side-lined and often ignored by Muslim couples today, but that is very much part of our traditional legacy. The *nikah* contract outlines a couple's expectations and conditions of living within a marital relationship: each spouse negotiates their roles and contributions. We drew up our *nikah* contract based on the Quranic verses that promote equality between spouses, as we wanted to base our relationship on the mutual love and mercy advocated in the Quran:

> "And among His Signs is that He created for you partners from among yourselves, that you may dwell in tranquillity with them, and He put love and mercy between your hearts. Verily in that are Signs for those who reflect." (*Surah* 30 Verse 21)

Besides these philosophical aspects of the contract, it also includes clauses on finances, education, child-care, and most importantly, divorce – more specifically, my right to initiate a divorce. In the years since I have become involved in women's rights activism, I have been faced with countless stories of women whose husbands refuse to grant them a divorce, of *ulemas* that refuse to annul marriages, even when women are being abused by their husbands. This simple clause in a *nikah* contract is a protective measure to ensure women never have to be so humiliated and dehumanised by their husbands and so-called religious institutions. In addition, the contract includes the right to seek a *faskh* (in our case, from a scholar whom we both agreed on) and a *khul*.

Educating women about these different types of marriage dissolution is imperative. For too long, men have been taught that they hold the power of divorce solely in their hands, to dispense with at will, and they dangle this perceived authority – the 't-word'* – over women with impunity. The purpose of negotiating and stipulating divorce processes in a marriage contract is not because we want marriages to end, but to educate and empower women about their rights, as well as to educate men about the correct procedure of marriage dissolution – which is one of mediation and counselling, not simply shouting out, "*Talaq!*". I also negotiated my *mahr* – I did not want it to be a mere symbol (although some women are happy with this, and that's their prerogative), but rather a true investment for me, especially for the years when I would be pregnant and nursing. In addition to this, we later married in a civil union, carrying our *nikah* contract over, and again ensuring the just and fair distribution of assets.

I cannot stress enough the importance for new couples of drawing up a *nikah* contract. Just the process of writing it up together is enlightening and an exercise in getting to know your partner! On the other hand, I cannot claim that a *nikah* contract alone will magically solve all the problems that can and do arise in marriages – it will not. Love, trust and commitment are not guaranteed by merely signing on the dotted line. Disagreements, arguments and incompatibility are not averted by a document. What a marriage contract can provide is a way to understand each other at the outset, as well as ensuring legal protection and religious rights. It is also a stepping stone to building a strong relationship based on faith in a Just and Compassionate God.

My husband already had experience in political and student activism, so he easily took my constant questions and debates in his stride, and as a couple we both began to express and embody equality in our day-to-day lives. This aspect of our relationship was accentuated when I gave birth to twin girls six years ago: this is when the true work of equality starts – in the night-time pacing, early morning nappy changes, bedtime routines and all the labours of love that go into raising a family. I am a firm advocate of couples moving away from mothering and fathering roles that place them in completely separate universes, towards co-parenting, so that each spouse can be empowered to fulfil her or his own life's purpose and dreams. It is only in a home where domestic and child-care responsibilities are shared that this can be a reality. Yes, I do believe men need to step up to the role of caregivers and nurturers – they are more than capable.

My life's work took me to academia – research, writing and teaching on Islam – rather than to a financially driven career. I am so grateful to my husband, Ebrahim, who makes it possible for me to follow my passion for activism and knowledge. I am proud to be married to a man who supports me in every way, including financially, whose entrepreneurial spirit makes so much of what we do possible, who is so committed to our *rizq*. Even while he juggles the time needed for his own social activism, he still comes home to take over caring for the kids; lightens his workload when I'm travelling;

and stops everything except fathering when I'm teaching, attending conferences, doing research or have speaking engagements. I am not in the slightest way ashamed to be financially reliant on such a man, because I know with certainty that my contribution to our family and community is in no way lesser or inferior to his financial contribution to our family.

As a self-identifying Muslim feminist, I believe that gender equality in a marriage is not about who puts bread on the table; it is about how. When it is done gently, with humility and in service to the family, not with a sense of propriety and superiority; when all decisions are made together and in consultation, regardless of who the breadwinner is; when there is transparency; and when the financial provider genuinely seeks to secure and empower his/her spouse – that is equality. Couples who can internalise this principle will also understand that all contributions to the family unit are important, and that bringing in the money does not absolve one of domestic responsibilities, nor does it require the spouse responsible for more of the domestic matters to be indifferent and oblivious to financial affairs.

Striving for a marriage that is rooted in equality is not always easy. There are many challenges along the way, especially societal and family expectations, which weigh heavily on our subconscious, as well as the way we have been socialised since birth into gendered stereotypes about who should be doing what in a marriage. You have to learn to simply stop caring about what other people think and focus on what works for your family. Equality is not the goal of marriage, it is a framework, and there are times of compromise and conciliation.

In my experience, gratitude and acknowledgement are key ingredients to a successful relationship: expressing sincere appreciation for each other's contributions and honouring each other's sacrifices and achievements. A marriage built on higher consciousness brings blessings and contentment into the home. Praying, reflecting on the Quran, engaging in *dhikr* and being in nature together, as well as creating the space for your spouse to have uninterrupted time alone for spiritual practice and pursuing her or his interests are all ways to live in peace and harmony with each other.

By no means is our marriage perfect, but neither are we trying to have a perfect marriage – if such a thing exists. As two individuals, two egos living together, we can never expect constant harmony, but each time we privilege our higher selves, our souls (which are essentially the same in every human being – all a breath of the Divine) we are able to let go of petty, trivial disagreements and laugh at the molehills we make into mountains. Having a common approach to serious problems is also essential, as well as agreeing on trusted friends, mentors and scholars to turn to for advice.

On a community level, we face huge challenges on the issue of Muslim marriages in South Africa. Muslim marriages are not yet recognised by South African law; however, Muslim women scholars, lawyers and activists are constantly working towards a just Muslim Marriage Bill that challenges patriarchal and hierarchical interpretations of Muslim family law. In too many families, women who work and contribute financially to the home are still expected to fulfil all the traditional domestic responsibilities, while juggling their professional lives. Muslim women are still refused divorces, financial compensation for their contribution to their marriages, equal distribution of assets and child-care maintenance. Domestic violence is rampant in our community and shrouded in silence; affected women are often counselled with *sabr* by religious leaders – a perversion of the beautiful spiritual practice of perseverance. Emotional and spiritual abuse is seldom considered as oppressive.

As Muslim women, we need to start speaking out for ourselves and for each other, so that no-one is allowed to suffer in silence and told to tolerate oppressive situations as an act of piety. Our very definition of human dignity must change so that, as individuals, couples and community we can start living as the Quran tells us to live – as *awliya* – helpers, intimate friends, supporters and mutual guides: "The believing men and believing women are *awliya* of one another" (*Surah* 9, Verse 71).

* The 't-word' refers to talaq (divorce).

Planning for the marriage vs planning for the wedding

Adela Bootha

From the time I was 12 years old I wondered whom I would marry. Would he be tall, dark and handsome? Would he have an extraordinary and exciting career? Would he be romantic? Would he be funny and charming? Or would he be just plain and simple?

And then, in a blink of an eye, my wedding day arrived. It was both bittersweet and scary. My husband met all my expectations and more. He was tall, handsome, interesting, well-educated and sweet. But I didn't really know him; in fact, I had no idea what it would be like to run a home with him.

I had lost my mother to cancer when I was 20 years old. That meant that there was going to be no one to call when my rice dish went wrong or when I needed guidance on certain in-laws' protocols. Learning the hard way was what marriage was going to be all about.

My father had always been open and frank in his discussions with us siblings, and his countless stories always had life lessons in them. But no number of conversations prepared me for another whole family that was different from my own and for living with a man whom I adored, but who was brought up differently from me.

As time went on, my husband and I realised that we had similar goals but we followed different paths to get there. Similar ideas, but different approaches. Similar needs, but different interests. My way always seemed best to me, and to him his way was better. While none of these differences were catastrophic, it still meant that nurturing the marriage required much hard work, patience, maturity and nerves of steel.

While attempting to navigate the maze of our marriage, in another blink of an eye our three beautiful, yet even more challenging children arrived. The dynamic of the marriage relationship changes when children arrive: communication channels with one's spouse are sometimes limited to texting, e-mailing and having a shared calendar, in order to keep up with appointments, invitations and other important dates.

If the relationship between the couple has not been established with mutually agreed rules, roles and an acceptable means of communication before the children arrive, one can forget about a smooth transition to having energetic children, who always have very important stories that constantly take preference over any adult conversation.

Unfortunately, no one warns us about what is to come and many of us are flung head first into the bizarreness of it all. We reason that we all come from good families, and we KNOW that our own family will be even better. We will be more efficient, and we will have little angels for children. Really?

Over the years a marriage goes through many phases, both with one's partner and his family and with one's children. It takes more work than one ever realises.

Oh, wait! Did I even mention wanting a career? And what about wanting to be good at it! That is another whole chapter.

With all this said, how can we better prepare ourselves for "a happily ever after"?

The answer to that is pre-marital and marriage counselling.

Common misconceptions, leading couples to avoid pre-marital counselling are:

"My dad, aunty, neighbour knows the boy's family well."

"He is a wealthy man."

"She comes from a good family."

"We have been dating and we know each other by now." (Un-Islamic, yet it commonly occurs).

"We have spoken to each other on the phone or via text message every day since he's proposed."

"My family has done a background check on his/her family."

None of the above-mentioned statements can fully prepare one for marriage. What you see in a potential spouse before marriage is usually very different to what happens in the relationship after the *nikah*. This leads me to the phrase I've heard on numerous occasions, "He/she was never like this before we got married!"

Pre-marital and marriage counselling is rather about aiming for a successful marriage, wherein:

- Compatibility is achieved;
- Perceptions are debunked;
- Expectations are negotiated;
- Interests are consented to;
- Needs are comprehended;
- Goals are approved;
- Decision-making processes are established;
- Personality is understood; and
- Mutual respect is gained.

This is concluded through a process of exploring areas such as finances, religion, roles and responsibilities, health, children, family, friends, children, romance, etc., as well as, in some cases, undertaking psychological assessments.

For a decision so big, one that will affect us the rest of our lives, that we will have to face every day, it is worth investing time in ensuring that the relationship is wholesome, before we even start planning for the wedding.

The importance of a marriage contract
Papatia Feauxzar

A marriage contract, also known as *nikah*, is an Islamic right that is often circumvented and discounted in many Muslim communities. In Islam, one cannot be considered to be married if an Islamic marriage contract didn't take place. As such, this contract should have reasonable and valid stipulations to it. Now, the trend is that many Muslim communities deter Muslim women from making any stipulations other than the dowry they are rightfully entitled to. In my opinion, it's not right to bully a bride into not making any additional demands in her Islamic marriage contract, because, then, consent is not uniform from both parties, and, predictably, this will provide the basis of many disagreements in the life of the couple. The bride will certainly become highly resentful, due to the fact that, indirectly, a choice was made for her.

From experience, I have learnt that, while some men are God conscious, they will discount a grossly important part of the Islamic marriage or contract. For instance, they will get away with not honouring your *nikah* rights, if you let them! One such discount takes the form of suggesting the bride should gift her dowry back to the groom. While gifting your dowry is an honourable thing to do when not asked to, it borders on bad faith and avarice when your future husband pressurises or tricks you into not claiming your rightful reward. Like a close married friend says, "Booty ain't free!"

Having said all that, the dowry is not the biggest problem underlying marriage contracts. The dowry is used as a distraction; many Muslim women find themselves looking in the wrong direction when it comes to *nikah*. Instead of discussing dowry amounts, they should rather discuss the marriage, because that's more long lived than the dowry, which will probably be spent in a blink of an eye. You won't be married for a blink of an eye, trust me. So what I'm saying is, while keeping an eye on your dowry, don't lose sight of your future living arrangements, wants and needs in the whole process.

My marriage contract didn't include any stipulations besides the dowry amount that was due to me. However, all my stipulations were discussed with my husband-to-be and agreed upon before the day we got married. We met online and lived in different states in the USA. I felt that I was getting old with no attractive prospects at 26. So I went on an online matrimonial site to find a Muslim husband. He was also looking for a match there. We clicked instantly, and started communicating. For several months we just exchanged e-mails. But we never talked on the phone or heard each other's voices until we actually met, with his parents present.

My husband first suggested that we move to Turkey to live with his parents. I refused to, because I had seen the negative results for family and friends who had lived with their husbands' families in Ivory Coast, Africa, where I am originally from. We then debated which state to live in, in the USA. My husband wanted me to move to where he lived. I couldn't agree because of my working visa requirements at the time.

I flew to Maryland and the *nikah* was performed on a brisk Thursday night in mid-November with people I barely knew. My family wasn't there but we had witnesses. A *nikah* was also done for us in Ivory Coast, my birth country, at the mosque, with my uncles and relatives. When she visited, my mother brought a Muslim and Ivorian official marriage licence, together with the video footage of the event. I was protecting my interests everywhere I saw fit!

It was five months later before we got married officially by the rules of the land. I had encouraged my husband to get a non-Islamic marriage licence as well, which is important, because we live in a widely secular society, with certain rules we have to abide by. I wanted my Islamic marriage to take place on the same day my secular union was officiated, but because my husband hadn't gone to the county clerk to get the secular licence, we only did the *nikah* marriage that day. I didn't give up, so, after being married for five months, we both took a lunch break from work, and, within an hour we had said our vows before the Justice of Peace, with nobody else present, and we were officially married under Texas Law.

After almost six years of marriage, I lived with my in-laws for one month while my husband went for Hajj, and – there is no simple way to say it – it wasn't easy, even though I love them dearly. It was tough, and it verified my suspicions all along. After having dodged the experience for so long, I couldn't delay staying with them for a short while. If something happened to my husband while he was on Hajj, being with his family was his way for my son and me to be cared for.

Before he left, we put all our finances in order and laid out all of our plans. We had the deepest discussion in our marriage to date. I felt secure knowing that if anything happened, my non-Islamic marriage licence would allow me to earn life-insurance proceeds from my husband's workplace. Although these decisions were not included in my initial marriage contract, we have an open line of communication in my marriage, which allows for such decisions to be made.

In our pre-marital negotiations my husband stated that he did not want me to study further when we were married. At that time I did not say, "Yes, I agree" or "No, I disagree." After being married for two years, I enrolled for one class towards a Master's degree in Accounting and judged his response. I made sure I did all my chores. Otherwise, my negligence would have been used as 'ammunition' against me. When he did not complain, I registered for more classes, as I was determined to graduate in one year with my Master's in Accounting, and I did, *alhamdullilah*. In that last semester, I almost died of exhaustion by taking not one or two or three, but five classes. Now, I'm studying further and my husband has paid for my fees. I hope to embark on a PhD soon, *Insha'Allah*. When it comes to my own success, I will not take no for an answer!

It needs to be remembered that a marriage contract is always under revision. If you are already married, and didn't get an Islamic marriage contract or a legal contract, strive to get one, or negotiate new terms that will be enforced. And if you are still negotiating marriage and have not stipulated your demands in your marriage contract, make sure that when you sit down to discuss the marriage with your future husband in the preliminary meetings – chaperoned or not – you state your demands clearly, giving reasons for what you want.

Above all, there will always be challenges in a marriage and in life in general. But what's life without them? I would say plain and boring! Keep negotiating.

4

Words of wisdom from my *Naani*

Safiyyah Sujee

Anybody who knows me knows that one of the most colourful characters, yet a pillar of strength in my life, is none other than dear old *Naani*, my maternal grandmother. Don't ever underestimate her thinking. She may look like a fragile, quiet little old lady, but she will put you in your place the moment you step out of line, and then two minutes later she will be spoiling you with her world class, finger-licking-good *akhni*, homemade jam and scones and her famous trifle dessert, over a discussion filled with golden pieces of advice.

I am 25 years old now and unmarried; my grandmother's greatest nightmare, which currently makes me her supreme mission in life. She wasn't at all concerned about my younger sister, who married well at the age of 21, making my battle all the more challenging.

"You must stop being so picky," *Naani* said one day as we sat together on her wooden dining room set, enjoying mangoes on a warm Durban summer's day.

"But *Naani*, nobody really interests me. If they're good looking they're players, if they're smart, they're arrogant, if he's well to do, he's not the brightest crayon in the box and triple-dipped in psycho, there are so many weird guys out there," I retaliated.

"What weird-weird? What about all the boys that probably find you so weird? No. You must behave nicely and be polite. Smile when they talk to you; don't act like a *jungli* woman."

"Hmmm..."

"You must worry about character and *akhlaq*, not how many BMW he got, how many phones he got, what bicycle he got and how famous he is in the YouTube and the WhatsApp, that's not important."

"*Jee, Naani.*"

"He must be a boy that will look after you, doesn't matter if he isn't rich, today people are rich, tomorrow they lose everything then what will you do? Grow together. Make sure he prays *salaah*."

"*Jee, Naani..*"

"And very important...he must have a good backside."

She didn't even flinch. *Naani* just made that comment absolutely straight-faced and in total seriousness. Oh my, is she joking? How do I even respond to that? What has this world come to? *Naani* is asking me to make *zina*; is that how she chose *Naana*?

"He mustn't have very bad habits, good family."

She continued on and on, until I finally realised she meant background. Backside was actually background, what a relief.

I gained some interesting insights that day, after my near heart attack. Some of her advice resonated with me and I hope to apply it in a real-life situation someday.

Growing old together was something that *Naani* advised as important. She strongly advised against pre-marital relations. Her reasoning made pretty good sense to me; people only learn to know each other to a certain extent before marriage. Even if they have 'known' each other for years, being married is an entirely different ball game. The first few months of marriage generally tend to be very challenging for most couples, for good reason. Two people from different families, histories, values, methods and possibly even different traditions come together and now have to merge into one, and this requires effort, compromise and a great deal of patience.

What made even greater sense, following *Naani*'s advice, is that dating and getting to know one another over a long period of time, contrary to common belief, actually lengthens and complicates the process. Prior to marriage, every person puts their very best foot forward – spoiling, smiling – and butterflies are the order of the day. They wear their best clothes and are always obliging and respectful. After marriage, even couples who have been dating for a long time discover new things about their spouse that they were unaware of. The process of adapting to being married is lengthened, rather disappointing and more emotional, because prior to marriage everything appears to be different.

Naani explained that allowing love to grow after nikaah means that you learn to love the person as they are, with all the flaws, getting the real deal, instead of a pre-painted picture of perfection and romance. Beautiful, really. Allah is so wise in all that He has condemned and allowed for us. The Quran prohibits *zina* and fornication. I always imagined that I would marry someone I know, have worked with or have had some time to get to know, but now, after *Naani*'s advice, I know that the very best, as well as *halaal*, option would be to allow love to grow after marriage.

Further to that, it is a universally accepted concept that women need love more than anything else, and men require respect. Probably one of the only things more fragile than glass is a man's ego. Injure his pride and you could unleash the ugliest side of a man. *Naani* advised clearly and sternly – learn to be quiet in moments of anger, don't insult your husband, and never lash out when he's just returned after a long day. Look good, smell good, greet him amicably, and, once he is rested, in a calmer mood and more comfortable you can bring up your concerns and worries in a rational and composed manner. You will achieve so much more than having let a tired, hungry and stressed man hear your day's complaints and troubles. Agreed, it takes a great deal of patience and composure to do this, but the rewards are wonderfully sweet.

On that warm afternoon, in between putting her mango peels in the dirt platter and picking up a fresh slice, *Naani* explained that, even though the saying goes that the way to a man's heart is through his stomach, it is even more so through his mother. Take care of and love his mother, as this will increase his affection and respect for you. She went on to tell me that a wife should also look after her husband's money and not spend frivolously. He will feel happy that she appreciates his efforts to contribute financially, and that she cares enough about his contributions to watch her own spending.

Suddenly I was alerted to the call of the *adhan*; it had already been an hour since *Naani* started handing out her pearls of wisdom. I often wonder what my life would be like, without *Naani*'s invaluable advice. Funny thing is, sometimes I feel that she is exaggerating and that I know better, and then some time later, her words echo meaningfully in my mind. I hope that someday I have the opportunity to take heed of all the treasures she has handed down to me, and can reflect back on my life with pleasure, not regret.

5

An ideal world...
Mariam B. Daya

When you were a little girl, you probably played 'house'. You pretended to be a mother, and even a wife, cooking up strange plastic items, sweets, or even mud cakes. You took care of your dolls and other toys, making sure they were fed, and that they behaved. Your cousin or neighbour played the husband who returns after a long day of work, wanting dinner to be on the table. Excitedly, you put the concoction before him, and together you both enjoyed this 'play-play' wedded bliss...

I remember when I was about ten; we cousins would talk about weddings and getting married. We'd decided that the oldest of us would get married first. Although we acknowledged it might be the prettiest, as there would be more interest there, we could never decide who the prettiest was, so the oldest held rank. After having made this decision, we paged through magazines, thinking about what outfit suited each of the rest of us. Naturally, white was taboo, as it would copy the bride – a big no-no! The older cousins had freedom of choice, whereas the youngest would have to settle for the dress no one wanted. In this lottery, I was fortunate to get second choice. Once the outfits were sorted, the décor and food were selected; *biryani* being the preferred meal. All that was missing was the groom. Life was ideal, life was simple, and everything was going to work out... More often than not, though, life takes you down an unexpected path. It's not always well paved, rarely has good lighting, and there's very likely something lurking around every corner.

I was about eighteen when I was set up for my first '*samoosa* run'. It was nerve wracking, an experience I wished never to repeat. But, alas, since he was not 'the one', I would have to.

A few more *samoosa* runs followed, with no real interest from either side. They just elevated my anxiety levels.

"Don't worry, you'll definitely find your guy," I was told, even though I had started disbelieving it.

"Keep an open mind."

"Don't be too fussy."

"It's okay if he's shorter than you."

"Why do you keep saying no?"

"Nobody's perfect!"

Everyone voiced their opinions, but hardly anyone asked me how I felt. As if the continuous disappointments were not enough, I had developed a chronic condition. It left me feeling tired all the time, because I rarely got a good night's sleep. It caused me pain and suffering, especially if I did not take care of myself. Medications seldom worked, and even if they did, it was only for a short while.

"When someone comes to see you, don't tell them you're sick," people advised. I wasn't that sort of person, so I intended to play with open cards.

Soon after, I had another *samoosa* run. The meeting went well; like, really well, even after my 'confession'. He seemed kind and sweet, and he was tall! I was nervous and scared. After the official proposal came, I read my *istikhara salaah*, praying for guidance. Was he the one? Would he accept me, despite what was wrong with me?

I received no clear answer, but my mother told me that if I wasn't against it, I should say *bismillah*! In other words, yes. This was it; I was going to take the leap. I prompted my mother to clarify that they understood my condition, and that they were alright with it; at least before she revealed my answer. So that night, she called Mr Eligible's mother, who said that they would need to discuss as a family and they would get back to us. It didn't sound promising. I had never heard of such a thing happening before.

A day or so later, the proposal was retracted; they apologised, and were never heard from again. Their outright rejection was shocking, and more than a little disheartening. It hurt. Remember, I mentioned things lurking around every corner? Well this thing had a club!

After some time, I understood. I couldn't blame them. Perhaps he was never 'the one' to begin with. I didn't want to go through the stress of any more *samoosa* runs, or the pain of rejection again, but I had little choice. I managed to keep it limited, though, so as to get back up every time I was knocked down.

"Don't worry, you will find your guy."

A few years on and another *samoosa* run later, I met an interesting Mr Eligible. We seemed to get along really well, until he asked me if my condition was hereditary or genetic. I knew this to be a darkened alleyway. At that point, things began to seem desperate...The walls closed in and suddenly began to collapse around me.

"It doesn't matter whom you marry, as long as you get married!"

I was horrified when I heard those words... And coming from a family member made it so much worse! Why would you say something like that!? Was being married the only end game!? Was my worth determined solely on my relationship status? Ah, but such is life...

In an ideal world, things would have gone exactly as my ten-year-old self imagined. But here I am, a number of years later – unmarried. If you thought this story was going to turn out differently, I apologise. I'm not sorry, though, about everything that's happened. My ordeals have made me stronger and perhaps a little wiser. It took me a long time to realise that my worth is not determined by any human relationship. The only relationship that really matters is the one with Allah.

Life keeps throwing curveballs. But see: now I have a baseball bat of my own. So, if you're not married yet, or if you think you might never be, don't despair. Things can change at any time. In the meantime, work on being a better you, and improve your relationships with others. It's not always easy, but you will get through it.

I have thought about what I would like in a husband. I would like my husband to be kind and sweet, and of impeccable character. I envision him to be funny, understanding, smart, strong and determined. And, of course, tall! He must be steadfast in his connection with Allah. I would love for us to cook and wash the dishes together.

I believe a marriage is a partnership, but it doesn't always go fifty-fifty. Sometimes one has to put in a little extra effort, and sometimes the other has to compromise a little more. Occasionally, you will experience more give than take. The foundation, as my mother says, should be rooted in honesty and trust. Respect, too: that's important! Perhaps, in an ideal world, this knight in shining armour does exist, but in the real world, who knows...Maybe, life keeps beating him off the path, or giving him distracting quests; so much so that his mettle is being tested. If it had not been so, what sort of knight would he be...?

I can't advise you on what to expect when you get married, but if you're waiting, or if you're about to take that next step, I can share with you advice that I keep hidden in my 'bottom drawer', together with the rest of my trousseau:

Keep your heart open, but also your eyes. Don't get married simply because you're lonely, or people are looking down on you for not being married.

If you're having problems, don't think marriage will solve them.

Hold steadfast to your principles, and, while everyone has to make compromises and sacrifices in their lives, don't always be the one doing so.

No matter how much you think you know someone, you don't really know them until you've lived with them.

Financial stability is important but it will never be enough to sustain a relationship.

Make sure he prays *salaah*. If he doesn't make time for his Creator, how will he make time for you?

Take your husband's family as your own: love them and respect them. Lose the preconceived notion that your mother-in-law is evil; that isn't her default setting. Try getting to know her before you decide you hate her. Treat your husband and in-laws the way you would want yourself and your own family to be treated. In other words, before making assumptions, try and understand things from their perspectives. Not everyone was brought up the way you were. If something bothers you, and it will, try not to get angry and yell; instead talk about the way you're feeling and why.

Express gratitude and love. Appreciate even the little things. It's not going to be smooth sailing, things go wrong, life happens, but together you can overcome it.

Marriage should not be taken lightly. While there is the fun stuff, it involves a whole lot of work!

Lastly, you'll get advice from many people and some of it won't always be good for you. Learn, and adapt it to your truth.

If you're ready for the step into marriage, and are about to take it, I wish you well. If you are yet to find your Mr Eligible, try not to worry too much. Everything will happen in its time. Live your life and be happy. This isn't an ideal world, but it's still pretty amazing! Make the most of it and remember, as Rumi said, "What you seek, is seeking you..."

Pearls of wisdom

• •

Prepare for your marriage more than you prepare for your wedding. The marriage is forever, the wedding is one day. Find a reputable counsellor who will assist with pre-marital guidance. This is not to dissuade the couple from getting married, but rather to assist with the transition going forward. **Adela Bootha**

Too many young people go into marriage these days with no understanding of the kind of maturity that is actually required! Women need to be smart and savvy to survive and establish boundaries early on. There are too many reports of abuse and extra marital affairs that result in the women being left with nothing emotionally and financially. Make sure that you and your partner are on the same page; small annoyances before marriage quickly steam-roll into an all-out war during marriage. People rarely change. **Razina Theba**

Best advice I ever received was from my cousin who told me on my wedding day that I should never let other people get involved in our private problems. We should always sort out our issues in our own home and never let anyone come between us. **Quraisha Dawood**

Communication and commitment are vital for a successful marriage. **Afzad-Al**

You will know when you are ready to get married when you can wholeheartedly and sincerely accept the fact that the only person that you can change is yourself.
Somayya Hansrod

Try not to have too many preconceived notions, opinions or expectations of others' marriages. Every marriage and couple is different. **Raashida Khan**

Nobody is perfect, but set high expectations for yourself, as well as for your husband. You can ask more of your partner if you are also doing everything you can to be a great partner.
Aneesa Bodiat-Sujee

Go into marriage without expectations and pre-conceived notions; and take each day as it comes. There is no manual for marriage, but if there was, my aunty would call it 'How to train a puppy'! **Waasila Jassat**

It's not about roses and coffees; it's also not all about you, so compromise. **Maymoonah Chohan**

FOOD AND MARRIAGE

Over time, a mythology develops around food. We see this in the culinary traditions passed on in cultures. Certain dishes are assigned celebratory status. Others are more suitable during convalescence or periods of mourning. Some are taboo. Stereotypes develop around which expatriate descendants from Indian villages prepare the best biryani. *It is the same in a marriage. Food becomes symbolised, codified. A shopping list of milk, bread, eggs and bananas signifies the day-to-day workings of the relationship. The bare bones stuff that keep the machinations ticking. There is nothing exciting about pancakes and omelettes, but they represent the quiet love of starting the day together.*

Saaleha Idrees Bamjee

Ways to the heart: Food in our marriage
Saaleha Idrees Bamjee

Whenever I hear people talk about the importance of compromise in a marriage, I think about mushrooms. I love their substantial earthiness. I love the way they reduce in a pan of butter, giving up their liquor, to become morsels of concentrated 'umaminess'. And I love the savoury meatiness of mushrooms when they're crumbed and fried. My husband, however, hates the stink and taste of them.

At first, I tried to excavate to the root of his aversion. Perhaps his first sensory experience was marred by a batch of fungus swimming in the cooking waters of their unrealised potential. Maybe he'd been scarred by a Sylvia Plath poem. I even went as far as to suggest that his mother or sister had failed him with sub-par mushroom preparation. As if I were dealing with a fussy toddler, I would surreptitiously add them to casseroles, only to find him picking them out and arranging them on the side of his plate like bullet cartridges after carnage. He will never be a mushroom man. I have made my peace with this. I did not marry him to change him. My own food quirk is my dislike of whole bananas. I can eat them blended in smoothies or baked into cakes, but the smell of the freshly peeled fruit nauseates me. Of course, the universe would steer me towards a man who eats a banana after most of his meals and who sometimes forgets to deposit the limp, blackening skin in the rubbish bin.

If I were to plot the significance of food in our marriage on a Maslow's Hierarchy of Needs pyramid, I would place it on one of the top tiers, somewhere between love/belonging and self-actualisation.

I like to think of cooking as an act of creativity. We cook to express appreciation or affection. It should not be a mandated chore, though I am not unaware of the general necessity of the task. There are days when meals are elaborate and inspired. There are also many days when supper is box fish and oven chips. On weekends, the kitchen is closed, apart from the occasional Sunday when I'm feeling particularly culinary. The important thing is that there is no pressure. If we are fed, however that may be, we are happy. That is the language we have developed together.

I never bought into the patriarchal approach that round *rotis* and a good hand with chicken *tarkari* signalled readiness for marriage. Surely, if a man wanted to eat well, he should buy his own copy of "Indian Delights"? But I happened to marry a feminist who can't cook. However, even though he comes from a lineage of men indulged by their mothers, he was that rare brand; the unfussy husband (except for mushrooms) who would never demand his orchestrated birth right of hot *rotis* straight off the pan for supper.

Over time, a mythology develops around food. We see this in the culinary traditions passed on in cultures. Certain dishes are assigned celebratory status. Others are more suitable during convalescence or periods of mourning. Some are taboo. Stereotypes develop around which Indian villages' expatriate descendants prepare the best *biryani*. It is the same in a marriage. Food becomes symbolised, codified. A shopping list of milk, bread, eggs and bananas signifies the day-to-day workings of the relationship. The bare bones stuff that keeps the machinations ticking. There is nothing exciting about pancakes and omelettes, but they represent the quiet love of starting the day together.

My husband doesn't like raw tomato in his take-away burger, but he often forgets to tell the server to remove it from his order. I like the taste of tomato slathered with mustard or mayonnaise and am more than happy to take the offending component off his hands. The tomato becomes a comfortable exchange, a nod that we don't have to enjoy the same things to like each other. Much like his glass of chocolate Nesquik that sits every morning on the same table as my cup of black coffee (always freshly ground, never instant).

Our eating oddities, some beyond mycophobia and problems with banana pungency, are personality markers. We accept these, along with snoring and a tendency towards messiness. (This applies to both of us: fortunately or unfortunately? I often wonder.) Our favourites become touch points; bonds formed over beef stroganoff and butter chicken. The heart soars over small affections, like me buying him chocolate muffins and him bringing home a bottle of the bitter malt that I like.

There is banter about whose mother makes the better mutton curry (mine of course, but his does an excellent *masala* chicken), but always with an abiding respect for these matriarchs. We recognise what our families have handed down to us and we fuse these inheritances to create something new. We do not have children yet, but are hopeful that there will come a time when we can pass on this mythology, building on it and creating new symbols and signifiers to tell a story that is uniquely our own.

Love, life and piping hot *roti*

Fatima Bheekoo-Shah

One of the first things my dad gifted to me after I got engaged in early Spring, 2001 was the orange "Indian Delights"* cookery book by Zuleikha Mayat. I remember him coming home from work just before *dhuhr*, and, tucked under his arm in a brown paper bag, was the book. He proudly handed it to me and told me it was my first wedding gift. The now tattered and torn book still stands proudly on my bookshelf and even though I hardly reach for it these days, it is one of my most treasured possessions. Thinking back, almost seventeen years later, he was not just handing me a recipe book, but a legacy of food and history, and perhaps a rite of passage of some sort. The book is a constant reminder of a father's love for his daughter, but perhaps also a gentle reminder that if I cooked well for my husband, my marriage would be happy.

I was in my early twenties then and by no means a newbie when it came to cooking. I had been cooking for our family of seven since I was thirteen. As a shy and awkward teenager, I had been thrust into the kitchen unceremoniously, while my mother worked in the family business. I would phone her countless times during those first tentative weeks, asking her exactly what I needed to do, and to make sure I had the correct *masala* combinations. I was not particularly worried about technique, because I had committed to memory most processes of cooking from watching my mother since the time I could reach the counter tops and see what she was doing.

While I avoided any social interaction, I threw my full, confident self into my kitchen adventures. Soon I was doing all the cooking, from the simple fish chutney and *roti* on Mondays to the big Sunday *biryani* lunch with all the trimmings. While I lacked self-confidence in other areas, I certainly did not feel any of that self-doubt when it came to food.

When it came to marriage, all I really knew as a young, naive woman was that my husband would never starve. I had grown up in a home where we had three meals a day, with tea in the late afternoon. My mom would cook a rice meal for lunch and for supper we sat down to hot *rotis* and a second type of curry. My dad seemed happy and my mom laboured away, sprinkling all her dishes with extra love and a dash of salt. It scares me to think this now, but at that time I did not think I needed much more in a marriage than my cooking skills. Many Indian women have this erroneous notion; it's something that is ingrained in us, not necessarily systematically, but, I think, from watching our own mothers.

While my family life centred on food, I married a salt-of-the-earth type of guy; the type of man who would happily eat meat and potatoes every single day and not complain. While he was not fussy, he was not really keen to explore new dishes. He wanted dishes he was familiar with. I wanted to experiment with new kinds of food, and although he never protested, my efforts were not given an overwhelmingly positive reception, either. Soon I got tired of impressing and I just reverted to cooking average, everyday meals.

Those early years were difficult, because, as much as I tried to appease our vastly different appetites in life, love and food, we were also still trying to find out exactly how we fitted in this union. I had hoped for my life to be similar to the Lady who served Prince Charming; the fable I had read countless times in "Indian Delights", and had romanticised in my head:

> "Each day, as soon as they had performed their evening prayers, he would commence to stroll around the block, giving her the time to lay out his dinner on the brass tray.
>
> Leisurely stroll over, he would arrive to enjoy his two hot curries, jug of iced water, pickles, and solitary, piping hot *roti* on the side plate. On the other half of the table, she was busy rolling out another *roti*, meanwhile checking and turning the one that was half done on the grilling plate. This way she replenished his *roti* plate with as many hot *rotis* as his massive appetite required ... Theirs was a tranquil home with little stress and no upheavals."

The old adage that a way to a man's heart is through his stomach did not apply to our marriage. And when this realisation hit me, it was a bitter pill to swallow. It took me a while to recover, but I finally realised that the Indian community places cooking on a pedestal, and, in so doing, we sometimes we forego essential components of a marriage.

I liken it to the layers of *biryani*, which often remind me of the layers of life. Each layer is prepared separately, with the utmost care. The onions need to be just the right shade of brown and the rice has to be boiled just enough, so that it does not turn mushy when you steam it. Each layer adds a depth of flavour and character. And even though the *masala* rice is mixed with the plain rice on our plates, we can still taste the difference. Most people will tell you that *biryani* tastes much better the next day. The flavours mature and mingle together, adding more depth to the dish.

It took me years, but I eventually realised that marriage is a lot like that. It needs time for the personalities and love to develop and mature. You won't figure everything out today, but, rest assured, by tomorrow there is more chance of you finding a better version of yourselves.

* "Indian Delights" by Zuleikha Mayat was first published in 1962.

Toasted cheese sandwiches
Safeera Kaka

Toasted cheese sandwiches. They are my favourite comfort food of all time. I can't remember my first bite of a toasted cheese sandwich. I do remember hearing my mother talk about working in Johannesburg city and enjoying the toasted cheese sandwiches at Koffiehuis. My father spoke about toasted cheese being the only food he'd order when he left our small town to do *hifz* in the big city. All I know is that nothing is more comforting than piping hot cheese, sandwiched between two slices of toasted bread. To me, it's soul food.

A toasted cheese sandwich is probably the first food I learnt how to make. My brother and I would conjure up our own breakfasts on Saturday mornings, while my mother and father were working. On school days, my beloved *daadi* would make them for us for school lunches, rather flat sandwiches with barely any cheese. In those days budgets were tight, but it was a delight, nonetheless.

Then came the diet days – months before my wedding – when I declared war on carbs and cheese, in an effort to get my generous frame into a more svelte state. But on mandatory cheat days, a toasted cheese made a satisfying breakfast.

A short while later, I found myself giddy in love, in a new kitchen, surrounded by a new family. A Sunday evening light supper was toasted cheese sandwiches. Bread was meticulously set out on a tray by my sister-in-law, my mother-in-law buttered the inside of the bread and a generous layer of cheese was added before the final destination, a hot frying pan. I marvelled at the different ways people do things, as I bit into half a sandwich with new-bride shyness.

Six months into marriage, gastro-type symptoms were diagnosed as an unexpected pregnancy. For four months, I struggled to get or keep anything down. I had the worst 'morning' sickness; morning sickness that lasted the entire day!

My appetite recovered in my second trimester, and all I wanted was toasted cheese sandwiches with loads of chilli. It was not an easy pregnancy. I lived away from family and friends and I felt scared and lonely. My familiar, but unwelcomed, companions, depression and anxiety, taunted me; but soon this all came to an end, when, a day before my birthday, I was induced and gave birth to my first child, a bouncing baby boy, after a long labour. I was delirious, in pain, exhausted, but content. The morning after I had given birth I enjoyed a cup of coffee and a toasted cheese sandwich. At that moment, life was perfect.

Three years after my son was born, my marriage stumbled into turmoil. Nothing brought me comfort or joy, not even my favourite comfort food. I agonised over whether or not my marriage was ending, and it tore me up inside. Eventually, we decided to fight for what we had, and embarked on a new chapter of our lives.

We bought our first home, I was a year into my work as a radio presenter (which I loved) and we started settling in as a family. I started to enjoy my new kitchen so much that I documented my gourmet creations on my social media pages. But gourmet or not, our favourite dinners in our sparsely furnished new home were toasted cheese sandwiches.

Life started to get busy, rollercoaster busy. I made toasted cheeses for my fussy eater of a son, on frantic mornings when I had run out of school lunch ideas (which were often). I'd also whip up a bunch of toasted cheese sandwiches when we had unexpected guests. It was the best food to enjoy on ice-cold evenings, in front of our cosy fireplace. It was the best food to enjoy, with copious amounts of tea and nourishing conversation, with my darling Z, a sister-in-law who became my closest friend. I came home and mechanically made a toasted cheese the day a doctor told me of the possibility that I would not be able to have another child. On hectic days, when I was the MC at an event and returned home late, I'd whip up a quick sandwich and sit down and tell my husband and son all about my day.

A little secret about toasted sandwich perfection: it has to be made at home. Fancy restaurants use unnecessarily fancy breads and cheese, and cheaper restaurants give you damp bread, filled with fake cheese.

In 2016, life hit me with another curve ball – grief. Losing *Daadi* was the most painful experience of my life. I remember days when I'd wait for my husband and son to go to work and school, so that I could crawl back into bed and cry till my head hurt. One morning, my housekeeper, Florah, came into my room. She quietly left a tray of tea and a toasted cheese sandwich as I lay sobbing on the bed. Honestly, it was one of the most touching gestures of my entire life. How amazing Allah is: even when He takes away the people we love, He blesses us with real-life guardian angels.

This is my ridiculous homage to a sandwich. Marriage, kids: these phases in life come with their ups and downs. Through the ebbs and flows of your life, I hope, like me, you can find comfort: in family, in friends, in Allah; and in a humble sandwich.

The taming of the shrew!
Hina Nafe

This tale is not an adaptation from Shakespeare's comedy, "The Taming of the Shrew". It is, however, a story about me; although I would argue that it is most unfair to call me a "shrew". Irresponsible? Probably. Immature? Not really. Lost in my own world? Definitely!

Unfortunately, though, "taming of the shrew" is the term my father used to describe to my future husband about what he had signed up for, by agreeing to marry me. I disagree with the description, and I'm hoping that my husband does, too, but I will leave you to decide for yourself by reading on.

A little about me, first! I studied to be a chartered accountant and the degree took five full years of hard work: sleepless nights studying for my exams, followed by working from morning to night to morning, to complete my mandatory training period. The routine that I rotated in did not leave time for anything else. Others considered me to be 'snobbish', for not attending social gatherings, a 'bookworm', for being engrossed in my studies whenever I was away from work, and 'lazy' for consistently escaping my chores.

In Pakistan, where I come from, girls who have mastered chopping onions, cooking curries and keeping the household neat and tidy are considered to be the successful ones. In fact, the most sought after ones for marriage are those who can keep their husbands' tummies happy with their skilled cooking. So, being a girl pursuing a career in something as challenging and as time consuming as Chartered Accountancy...you can imagine where I was ranked.

My mother managed all the household chores, with little or no domestic help from me. I, being the elder and only daughter, was supposed to help her; however, my mother never let me help until I was 17 years old, and, by that time, I was either too busy with studies or had become too lazy to help out. At most, I'd set the dinner table and wash a few dishes after dinner, and when she really pushed me, bake and cook a little. I did not manage too well; my attempts were a blend of the 'couldn't' and 'didn't want to' do it!

When the date of my marriage was set, it was my father who insisted that I help with the household chores. I was so hopeless that once, when my fiancé came over and requested a cup of black tea, I served him hot water in a cup, with a swarm of loose leaf black tea swimming on its surface. Being the gentleman that my husband is, he drank the whole cup without complaint. He reminds me of that incident every now and then, whenever he wants to emphasise how much he loves me.

Soon after the wedding date was set, I qualified and progressed to the next stage of my career. My working hours were a little more flexible, and so I had no excuse to escape the chores and learn the basics. I tried, but, to be honest, I never gave them my full attention. I was too busy trying not to think about having to migrate to another country after my wedding. My parents didn't give up trying to teach me, and it was then that my father tried his new technique of referring to our upcoming marriage as a "taming of the shrew" experience for my fiancé. He made sure he made this remark to him whenever I was around, hoping I would get embarrassed and take housework and cooking more seriously. Unfortunately, these tricks did not work.

The wedding happened and I embarked on my happily-ever-after journey, a 24-hour flight to New Zealand. Soon I found myself engrossed in a world of assorted spices and utensils. Like a child taken to a new playground, I was excited. I had been blessed with long, lonely days, as my husband worked long hours and I still hadn't got my work visa, so this gave me some time to experiment and learn. YouTube became my teacher. My husband played an important part, too, in my culinary lessons, as he ate whatever I presented to him, from burnt *chapatis* to watery curries.

Cooking was not my only nemesis; cleaning, laundry and ironing needed mastering, too. There were times in the early days, when I would revert to my old couch-potato self and ignore the looming chores until the last moment. Transformation for me did not come in one day!

It helped that my husband had exceptional cooking skills. No kidding! He had bragged about them before our marriage, and I had always thought he was exaggerating, but his skills were a lifesaver, especially when I was in my first trimester of pregnancy and couldn't stand the smell of cooking. He took it upon his shoulders to feed me, and for that I shall be ever grateful to him, and to Allah for blessing me with him.

When I started working, we spilt the tasks, with him mainly cleaning the house and me doing the rest. At times I was frustrated with him for not taking up cooking, since that was his area of expertise. I had to waste my Sunday mornings and afternoons cooking and freezing for the whole week, and then ironing took up the evenings. Little did I know that this was his way of boosting my confidence, making me self-dependant and helping me get better at house-related stuff.

Days went by, and he kept encouraging me, providing honest feedback and, sometimes, getting a little frustrated. I, on the other hand, fluctuated between being proud about managing to cook something good, feeling hurt when it turned out to be a disaster after so much effort, and feeling tired of the housework and routine.

We've been married for two years today, and I am an excellent cook now. I am managing a baby pretty much alone, since I don't have any friends and family here. The house is always clean, the laundry done on time, and so on. He doesn't have any complaints and that's what makes me happiest.

When I think back, I realise that perhaps it was a "taming of the shrew" experience for him, after all, but, thankfully, he never failed to encourage me and complained as little as possible. I wouldn't advise anyone to follow my path, though. Who knows what would have happened if my husband had been intolerant of my bad cooking, and had discouraged and made fun of my efforts from day one? Perhaps I would've been disappointed and given up. I tried, but he was the one who gave me the chance to try. He didn't just tame a shrew; he shaped an uncaring, lazy girl into a self-sufficient, all-rounder woman. My father now marvels at my miraculous transformation.

Food in a marriage
Afzad-Al

"A Mother says a way to a man's heart is through his stomach, her Son says it's the lower organ." (unknown)

Food – the preparation, presentation and consumption of it – has been a bone of contention in many homes across the world. According to Merriam-Webster, food is any nourishing substance that is eaten, drunk, or otherwise taken into the body to sustain life, provide energy, promote growth, etc. No food is ever going to be exactly alike. There'll be similarities, of course, but never the exact thing.

For, just as we cannot touch the same flow of water, no chicken, beef, vegetables or wheat are the same. Different crops yield different harvests.

That being said, it's amazing how mothers-in-law across the globe will all gripe about the same thing: "My daughter-in-law can't cook; my poor son."

Whether you are Indian, Italian, Portuguese, Zulu or Xhosa, the struggle is real.

As a South African Indian, this is my story. First and foremost, I am a Muslim woman and I'm proud of my heritage. Like most girls my age, in our youth we were expected to learn how to make certain dishes. You started out by doing 'grub' work: the cleaning, chopping, grating and washing up. It had to be done right the first time, or else there was hell to pay; most likely with a *velan*, or whatever your mother had in her hand at the time. There were no age restrictions; the earlier the better, or else, "What will the people say? Your mother didn't teach you?"

I started out at ten years old, and by the time I got married at twenty I was quite proficient in the kitchen, or so I thought. That all changed the day I became a daughter-in-law. I naively thought that being from the same *gaam* as the rest of the family, it would be a walk in the park. Ha! My innocence was robbed. I was one of four daughters-in-law. The competition and one-upmanship were totally alien to me.

From being a princess in my parents' home, I suddenly had to find my place. Never mind that I was still trying to get used to my husband and his family. The kitchen is another whole matter – you'll get some who don't eat what you prepare and stop their husband and kids from eating it as well, then there are others who don't mind what you cook, as long as they didn't have to.

I'm third-generation South African Indian; my great grandparents came from a village called Alipur in India. I mention this, as I strongly believe we take on certain characteristics and learnt behaviour from our parents and predecessors, especially with regards to food. My norm in our house was eating certain foods on certain days. For example, *biryani* was only ever served on a Sunday or a public holiday – always for a special occasion. My mum had a different *achaar*, pickle or condiment for every different food. (Yes, our fridge was stocked with many different kinds of bottles; it's a wonder we had place for other stuff.) Heaven forbid if you served these differently to how she wanted it. *Samoosas*, pies and other savouries were a weekly extra, sometimes daily. (I'm not talking about *Ramadaan* time.) That's besides the cakes, *chevro* and other traditional eats. The aunties would comment if you served tea with only one type of goodie. The host would be embarrassed and say that "the kids ate it all just before you came".

I grew up believing that a good housewife is one whose kitchen is well stocked, and naturally, everything is homemade. For the first few years of my married life I continued with that tradition. I was then forced to reassess and make changes.

I believe that we all bring something to the table (pun intended). Each woman is unique and comes with her own brand of knowledge, skills and talent. How we integrate our varied ideas makes all the difference. If we come in with an obsession to control, there will always be strife. Accept that there are many ways to prepare food, and that your way is not necessarily the right or best way. It's whether you make it with love and compassion that matters.

Food and its preparation are not gender based. It's been known from the time civilisation began that men are the hunters and women the nurturers, but in today's changing times, men are becoming master chefs, while women own the boardroom.

Food has a way of bringing people together. Instead of slaving away by yourself in the kitchen, outsource or delegate; that way, you can spend more quality time with your guests. Life is short: make memorable moments.

Marriage is a feast
Nabihah Plaatjes

"*Roti* not round: who's going to marry you?"

I chuckle to myself whilst scrolling through the newsfeed of a social media group and find this post that has an old Indian aunty carrying a *velan* and looking disappointed.

It's 9:30 pm and I'm trying to find inspiration for dinner ideas for tomorrow. As usual, my night prior to this entailed drama and a struggle that involved hair-pulling, crying, and a lot of asking for water...but I did it! I finally managed to put my toddler to sleep after the *esha salaah*, so now begins 'me-time'.

I continue looking through the posts on the group.

"Sweet chilli chicken; pot roast chicken with *aalo*."

Hmmm those sound delicious, but not for tomorrow, I thought. I love this group; they have such lovely ideas and different things to make. Why didn't I check the internet for dinner inspiration when I had just got married?

Still thinking about that funny *roti* post, I turn to look at my dear, sweet husband who is sitting next to me on the recliner, with his laptop on his outstretched lap, trying to finish the day's work before retiring to bed. As if on cue, he asks the usual 'wanting a snack while working' question: "Is there anything to eat?"

Although I feel quite perturbed, since I have just sat down, I realise that I wouldn't mind something to snack on for myself right now, too, so I hop off the couch and search through the freezer, looking for some cheese and corn *samoosas* for me and potato *samoosas* for him. We are in luck; there is just one dozen of each. You would think one dozen is a lot, but with our appetites, twelve *samoosas* can be eaten in one sitting, by one person!

As I pull out the frying pan and oil and begin frying the frozen savoury treats that were made by me, I think back to my younger years when my aunts used to tell me that I would soon learn how to make things that I never dreamed I would. They always related the story about how someone didn't even know how to make tea (not the type where you add boiling water from the kettle, but the type where you actually boil the tea on the stove and add spices) and now she makes pots and pots of the most mouth-watering and finger-licking food. They gave me hope, since my only way of cooking (before marriage) was buying already marinated meats and chicken from the butcher, popping it into the oven, and having it with ready-made *rotis*, *naans* or rolls.

"But didn't you learn how to cook curries?" Ziyaad asked, in our early stage of marriage.

"I learnt how to peel stuff," I scoffed, remembering those times when I was a young pre-teen and I wanted to help, but all I was asked to do was peel.

Peel and peel and peel.
I was bored of that.
Is this all there is to cooking?
What happens after peeling?
When's the other exciting stuff coming in?

"I didn't know much about spices," I told him. "I didn't feel privileged enough to make it to the next level and now, thinking about it, I would have loved to learn to decorate dishes of food, like the food stylists do. I recently saw that one stylist even made a bird's nest out of actual food items! These days, I also want to make food that's 'Instagrammable' or can be shared on Pinterest."

"Yeah, but it's one thing to have pretty food, and another to have food that actually tastes good," Ziyaad chimed in.

Annoyed, I muttered, "I was talking to myself."

"But I am your other half, so if you are talking to yourself, then you are talking to me as well!" Ziyaad replied. This guy and his comebacks! One day, when I have time, I will google witty comebacks and study them, so that I can also make snappy remarks when he speaks.

"Besides," I continued, feeling annoyed that we had gone off topic, "when I was in university and it was just my father, my brother and me, I used to cook – just not curries."

"Taking bought marinated meats and putting them in the oven is not cooking, you have to make a meal out of it. Like, what about vegetables? Add some yellow rice to it…" Ziyaad trailed off, and, feeling a bit sad, I went into full-on thinking mode. I realised that this was my chance to actually make a proper meal for a family that sits around together and eats together at meal times.

I remember our very first meal together after Ziyaad and I got married. His father and sister also lived with us and we had to set the table with a freshly made tablecloth, put placemats by each seat, lay down big plates, side plates, a glass, cutlery and a serviette for each meal. The food was then dished out from the pot into Corning Ware, and even bread and rolls were taken out of the packets and served on a plate. At each meal time! Every. Single. Day. Man, they used a lot of dishes! It was even worse that we couldn't afford a domestic helper.

"You guys eat like in a restaurant," I said.

They didn't understand my comment. How could they? They didn't know my background and didn't bother to ask.

During my first year of marriage, a lot of tribulations occurred, but these resulted in me learning more about different personalities, family and culture. I also managed to read more recipe books, both Indian and Malay.

My husband always mentioned something about a dish called *mavrou** that his late mother used to make, so I vowed to myself to learn how to make it. On his birthday, in our first year of marriage, I made it for him, complete with side dishes, all from scratch. He was completely taken aback, as he had no idea that I had planned on making this meal for him.

"*Mavrou!*" he exclaimed.

"Yes, I am your *vrou*," I winked, and grinned, as I thought that I had made the perfect witty remark. It was amazing to see the smile on his face, and, once he dug in and I could see that he was enjoying this particular cuisine, my heart felt content. The stomach really is the way to a man's heart, no matter what culture or race he may be.

My culinary learning didn't end there. It wasn't easy, but I tried my hand at savoury making, as our first *Ramadaan* as husband and wife was coming up. I wracked my brain, trying to remember the holidays I spent in a small town with extended family, including an aunt who used to make savouries for a living. Even though I used to feel painfully homesick, I learnt some valuable lessons whilst my cousin and I helped her to make all her goodies.

Soon, I was making curries and *breyani*, and I even made *rotis* and rolls! Sadly, my *rotis* were not round, at first. I can remember the first time I tried my hand at *roti*-making.

"Oh, sweet, you made *parathas*!" Ziyaad exclaimed.

My eyebrows came together in a frown as I saw him take the slightly crisped and square-shaped item and put it on his plate. Should I tell him that it was actually meant to be a *roti*?

He dished the mayonnaise-based chicken curry into his plate and began praising me through mouthfuls of food.

"Mmm, yummy."

Ever appreciative, I thought. Poor guy. He was born and brought up in Durban, and loved spicy food, so he thought he had scored when he married a real Indian girl who would know how to cook the curries that he liked. Unfortunately, for the first few years of our marriage, he had to get used to mayonnaise-based curries, as those were the only ones I felt comfortable making.

But now, here we are, sitting side by side and eating *samoosas* made by me!

With everything, practice makes perfect, and, although that might sound like a cliché, it really is true. Once you do something and keep on doing it, you learn how to improve on it, and it can only get better. Also, communication and honesty are the most important keys in a marriage, where two different families come together (in my case, two different cultures as well). Honest communication is the essential ingredient in the union.

* Cape Malay dish made with steak and spices; also a word that is very similar to the Afrikaans 'mevrou' (Mrs).

Those first 30 cups of *roti* dough...
Maymoona Chohan

When I took the bold step, I had all the romantic notions of marriage in my mind. I was even excited to live with 'in-laws'. Coming from a happy childhood and home, I thought marriage would just be a continuation of the same.

I wouldn't say I was in for a surprise, but, yes, life was very different.

Living with in-laws was not a problem. My parents-in-law were very happy to have me in their home. My husband had three siblings younger than him living with us, and even that did not scare me. I felt confident and honoured to be the older sister-in-law.

I am an optimist, so I took life in my stride, and I adapted to my 'new family' life without much fuss. There were differences in opinion and a few upheavals, but I kept motivating myself to believe that the situation would become better. After twenty years of being a happy-go-lucky person, I wasn't about to change into a miserable daughter-in-law.

The first year of marriage was definitely the most challenging, because I had to adjust to being a wife, daughter and sister. I tried my best to be 'nice' in all three aspects, but there were clashes. Even blood siblings have different personalities, so coping with five new personalities was a big challenge for me. I slowly learnt the likes and dislikes of the head of the house, my father-in-law, and tried my very best to always do things the way he liked. My mother-in-law made me feel very welcome in the home, and her acceptance made my new life easier.

Nonetheless, I remember some hilarious (and some not so, but these can stay unmentioned) episodes that went with adapting to living with my new family. Being the youngest in my own family, I had left the cooking to my sisters, and felt that my turn would come at a later stage in life. Advice that I always remember came from my own mother: "Learn while watching". Growing up in the days when there were no electronic gadgets, I spent a lot of time at home watching my mother, and also had the privilege of listening to her teach my sisters and cousin who lived with us. To this day, my cousin teases me about how I escaped the *'velan* lessons'.

My older sister-in-law got married four months after me, so it was after this period that kitchen duties became my responsibility. I was content with this responsibility, and because I worked only half days at that time, I thought that I would cook in the afternoons, when I came home from work.

To my surprise, one Saturday afternoon after we had had lunch, my mother-in-law announced that we would be cooking together for the week ahead. I argued that it wasn't necessary, because I would cook daily, but mother-in-law insisted that was the routine, so I agreed.

First things first; the helper was told to bring the flour for the *roti* dough. As a young child, I had watched my own mother make the *roti* dough with her bare hands every morning and I had marvelled at how she never burnt herself with the boiling water. When my mother mixed the dough, I would exclaim that the aroma from the *roti* dough did not smell good and declared that I would never make *roti* dough or *rotis*. I also did not eat *rotis*.

So, when the helper returned with a huge dish of flour, I asked my mother-in-law how many cups I should take out for the dough. My mother-in-law replied that we were going to make dough with all the flour in the dish: approximately 30 cups! I just stood there, shocked, as I knew that I was not equipped to make 30 cups of *roti* dough. I felt totally helpless. I remember relating the experience to my own mother later, over the phone. She did not say, "I told you so!", even though I knew that she wanted to. After that afternoon, I slowly grew accustomed to my mother-in-law's routine of cooking five pots of food and making 30 cups of *roti* dough on a Saturday afternoon. This ritual of cooking with my mother-in-law became the bridge to my acceptance into the family.

Another memorable incident that brings a smile to my face is my experience of my very first *suhoor*. My mother-in-law kindly asked me what I eat for *suhoor*, and assuming that every household ate the same thing, I politely replied, "whatever everybody eats". So, imagine my shock when I came to the table at *suhoor* to find a pile of buttered Marie biscuits! I was horrified, as I do not eat dairy products. Again, I related the story to my own mother, who advised me to tell my mother-in-law about my dietary requirements.

I realised over time that living with in-laws is similar to marriage; there is always give and take. I grew up with a personality that was different to those of my new family members and we had many disagreements over the 21 years that I lived with them. Disagreements are normal and form part of living with others. I am no angel and I do not say that I was the best there is, but, in retrospect, I realise that every situation can be dealt with tactfully and sensitively if you invoke the help of Allah. Communicate these disagreements to your husband but do not expect him to fight your battles. Try to see the situation from the perspective of others. Do not speak when you are angry, rather walk away and take time to reflect on the situation. Today, I try to pass on my life's lessons to my children, so that they, too, may learn from my experiences.

13

Cooked!
Khalida Moosa

I am the voyeur on the family recipes WhatsApp chat. I watch the ladies share and swap recipes on chicken tikka, Chinese *biryani* and flop-proof cakes, and pointers to Facebook sites with the fanciest desserts and easiest cooking hacks. None of this fills me with glee. Don't get me wrong, I love food: the consuming of it. And I'm not averse to appreciating great grub. But place me in a kitchen and ask me to feed the hordes, and I become a nervous wreck!

A few months before my marriage, Mummy would ask me to join her in the kitchen to observe and help out with the cooking. Invariably, I'd be in the middle of a good book. Her words to me, "I feel you sorry when you get married. How will you cook?" did not deter me from the exciting world of fiction that I was regularly immersed in.

I was confident that when I attempted to cook, it would come automatically and I would have a natural ability to do what so many women do with their eyes closed. After all, I had perfected baked beans with a tomato and onion base. Armed with this basic and my other culinary skill of making the perfect egg, we'd never starve.

Besides I had already warned my husband-to-be about my shortcoming in the art of cooking. He didn't seem to be too concerned. I felt pleased that I had been honest about the lack of this crucial skill.

Fast forward to my attempt at making my first chicken curry. I cannot remember if I consulted with a recipe book (did I even possess one?) or I cooked from intuition, but I knew immediately that something was not quite right. It didn't resemble anything my mother turned out. In fact, it looked downright unappetising! My husband returned from work and smiled proudly when I announced the chicken curry menu. He even praised my inedible effort. However, the meal didn't survive past the first bite. I gave the pot of curry to Agatha, my helper, to salvage. She, in turn, fed it to the resident dogs, which, to my relief, lived another day!

Being a reader, you'd think I'd be an ace at following recipes, package instructions, etc. Unfortunately I failed in this area as well. I recall making dumplings (from a recipe) THREE times, baffled that on each attempt they would not rise to the occasion. Eventually, after rereading the recipe, I realised that it called for self-raising flour, not the plain flour I had used.

My long-suffering family understand my handicap, although, now that I have kids, I do sometimes feel guilty that I short-change them. How else do mums the world over express their love, if not through skilful cooking? I have added to my baked beans and eggs repertoire, but will never reach the level of expertise all good Muslim women are expected to showcase. In rare moments, I feast my eyes on pictures in recipe books and feel a thrill of excitement. But soon enough, another culinary disaster occurs and this feeling dies down. Thank goodness for the ever-helpful home industries, which are never far away. After all, if it weren't for women like me, how else would they survive?

Food is not just about eating. It is what nourishes us and brings families together around the table at mealtimes, fostering an atmosphere of intimacy and love. I salute women (and men) who make this possible every day. For a long time, I was mortified to reveal my absolute disinterest in the art of cooking. After all, it is a rare breed of Indian woman who doesn't know how to roll a round *roti*, or put together a perfect triangle for a *samoosa* in record time. I have come to accept that I will not score an 'A' in a cooking course, nor will I be chosen for the next 'bake-off', and that's okay.

14. *Khidmat* in the kitchen

Aneesa Bodiat-Sujee

Going out in *jamaat* is almost like the boy scouts, I sometimes think: devout and dutiful wanderers; sincere spiritual nomads; travellers, intent on being covered in noble dust. Not all those who wander are lost. You must have a little streak of the adventurous in you, a taste for wanderlust: travelling from place to place with a backpack, relying on the hospitality of fellow Muslims and your own capacity to look after yourself, to survive in a strange place. This isn't a five-star vacation, though. If one of the uncles has smelly toes, you just make *sabr* and try to be cheerful.

People warned me that my husband may be "too holy" for me, that I might feel restricted by his lifestyle.

"What is 'too holy' anyways?" he asked.

There is no real way of judging a person's religious adherence. Most often, we humans are terribly bad judges of others. Yep, judging another's religious devotion is best left to the ultimate Judge, the One who knows our true intentions; the One who reads the pages of our hearts.

My husband tries to give time to the *masjid* every day, and he hopes to go out in *jamaat* for 40 days every year. Yes, he is a *saathie*, an 'old worker'.

I didn't know what to expect, at first. Initially, there's a whole new vocabulary to learn, Urdu words thrown around casually by the brothers, just part of their everyday vernacular: *chilla* (40 days), *saathie* (someone you've been out in *jamaat* with, your *jamaat* 'brother'), *kaal ghuzaari* (report back of your activities), *tashkeel* (invitation to come out with them on the path of Allah), *gasht* (the weekly visits to neighbourhood Muslims, encouraging people to come to the *masjid*), and on and on.

One of my favourite new words is *khidmat*. *Khidmat* means service. If you are 'on *khidmat*' for the day, you serve your fellow brothers, cooking the food, cleaning up, helping them with whatever they may need.

But what I love about the *khidmat* that my husband has learnt in *jamaat*, is that he brings those *khidmat* vibes home. I'll sometimes walk into the kitchen to find him finishing up the dishes, sneakily done while he let me sleep in. He likes to wield the biggest knife in the kitchen, chopping the onions to save me some tears. He knows what *vagaar* is, and he pays attention to the new vegetable recipe my aunt gave me – you never know, it may come in handy when he has to cook for his brothers. I didn't even know how to iron clothing when I got married, but my husband did, and he patiently taught me how. And when I get intimidated by a long, creased *kurta*, he steps in to save the day.

Ladies often complain that Indian men are momma's boys who have learnt nothing about looking after themselves in the home. I wonder if these stories of men unable to boil water for a simple cup of tea are true. If you don't do the laundry, will the guy wonder what magic happens in his mother's house, so that neat piles of clothes always appear miraculously in his cupboard?

I'm lucky. My husband travelled in *jamaat* for four months the year before we got married. He learnt self-sufficiency and the art of living simply. If you have to carry everything you need, you value experiences over things. You fix what gets broken and you understand how to fill every inch of your backpack efficiently.

My hubby gets irritated when people say things like, "We don't have to do this really, it's just a *sunnah*". Just a *sunnah*? My husband cannot bear dismissing the practices of the one who was sent to us as a guide, who worried about the future of his people, whom he would not meet on Earth. One of the practices of the Prophet Muhammad, may peace be upon him (PBUH), is that he mended his own clothes and helped with the housework. So *khidmat* ends up not only being a necessary skill learnt in *jamaat*, but, when applied at home, is the fulfilment of a *sunnah* as well.

Another useful practice of the *jamaat* that spills over perfectly into marriage is that of *mashwera*. There may be an *ameer* to lead and have the final say, but he should always consult with the group before making a decision. He must consider their views and take a decision after listening and weighing up everyone's opinion. Even with the simple act of, for example, buying a new printer, we have made *mashwera* a part of our routine, by consulting each other before adding more stuff to our home. If we practise with these little things, hopefully the discussions around the bigger issues, like how to raise our children, will become easy as well. It is said that a decision made after *mashwera*, whatever the decision is, is a good one.

I'm glad that I didn't take seriously the concerns of those who thought that a *jamaat* brother would be too sombre and restricting for my temperament. I have come to accept that I will never see my husband's naked chin. But that's okay with me. He talks intelligently about religion and he has a clear sense of how he wants to live his life. He knows where he wants to end up, ultimately, and he wants us to get there together. People still ask me how I knew that he was the right one for me. We made *istikhaarah* and asked for guidance. Also, he said that he wanted to make me happy. He does.

Apart from love and *barakah*, my husband has filled our home with the values of *khidmat*, *mashwera* and striving to follow the *sunnah*. He once gave me a bouquet of sharpened pencils. What more could a girl ask for?

15 "Hungry, darling?"
Raashida Khan

"Hungry, darling?" That's one question I always know the answer to. Not because I'm a mind reader, or so in sync with my husband, Zain, but because he is always hungry. Fortunately, he enjoys typical South African Muslim Indian cuisine, as that's what I've grown up eating and cooking, too. As in most of our homes, everything revolved around food. As a child, I was taught to respect and honour food. There was sufficient, even if friends and family dropped by unexpectedly (which was often), but never excessive, because wastage was frowned upon.

As the only boy in the family, with doting parents and three adoring sisters, Zain grew up spoilt. With good reason, as he really is the ideal son and brother. Early in my marriage, a friend commented that I was very brave to marry a man with three beautiful, talented sisters. I hadn't thought about it, and luckily, too, as I might have felt self-conscious or intimidated. The early years were tough, but, thankfully, we found our common place – food and eating!

Our shared love of food has been a unifier. If there is trouble in paradise, eating together can expedite the making-up. We try never to eat alone. I don't enjoy my meal half as much without him. This has cemented our relationship – dinner is a time to catch up on our days and the prelude to big or small events.

Zain and I have little rituals around specific foods or meals that are uniquely ours. I love dishing out his food, although most times, his mother has cooked. She lives with us. My in-laws have done so for years, even before my dear father-in-law passed on. This has been amazing for me, as I've learnt as much about cooking from Zain's mother (especially all his favourites) as I have from my mother, both of whom love cooking for him. Why not, when someone is so appreciative?

Zain loves grilled prawns but hates peeling them, a task I happily do for him, not least because I enjoy licking the marinade off the shells. I adore dark chocolate and I always have a variety in my bedside drawer. While I do most of the shopping, that is one thing he buys for me. I never enjoy my night-time treat as much if I purchase it myself. Zain intuitively knows when my chocolate stocks are running low and replenishes them in good time. Similarly, he favours gums (he has an extremely sweet tooth) and has a stash that I'm responsible for in his pedestal drawer.

On a recent visit to my mom, I offered him a choice of strawberry, salted caramel, chocolate chip or guava flavoured yoghurt for breakfast. He grinned and said, "Why are you asking? You know what I like." I did. I always do.

I'll share a secret with you. I can influence his mood (no, no, you didn't read 'manipulate him!'), by what is served and in what sequence. I've learnt to time my requests at crucial junctures while eating, but please, let's keep that between you and me, okay?

Zain loves watching me eat, because I relish and savour every bite. It may sound like an over-simplification of my accomplished, intelligent husband, but I swear that's when he's happiest. This has extended to our sons as well. Nothing pleases him more than for us to enjoy a meal together. When I've picked up a few kilos, it's invariably his fault.

Ours was an arranged marriage – the modern kind, where potential spouses are introduced and the decision to marry theirs. We were lucky – we got along, and, in a few short months, were married. Nine months to be precise, during which time we hardly saw each other, because Zain lived in Johannesburg and I was still in Durban. There was a long telephone call every second evening and Zain visited over a couple of weekends, when we had some opportunity to spend time together; never alone, though. Those were the days before the proliferation of cell phones, so we didn't have constant communication and blow-by-blow accounts of our days. So, we only really got to know each other and learn to love one another after we were married. I know the exact moment when it became truly, madly, deeply in love, for Zain. It was the first time I cooked *khuri kitchri*, with the works. He took his first bite. His eyes glazed over sublimely and he looked like he could devour me as heartily as he was going to polish off his plate, but priorities, priorities – never let the food get cold!

"I love you, Raashi," he said in between mouthfuls of crispy *aalo* fry, *aamli* peppers, fried fish and freshly chopped *kachumber*. "You make me soooo happy." This was even before I perfected the art of *mithai* making – *burfee* and *laddoo* are his favourites, but he is partial to my other sweetmeats. Oh, did I mention the pancakes and mealie fritters that are a standard accompaniment to Sunday morning breakfast?

Don't let all this fool you. I was and still am fiercely independent. As a younger woman, I considered myself a feminist, and I still ascribe to those values: I would now call myself a woman first, then a wife and mother after. As a newlywed, I wanted to incorporate equality into my marriage. I discussed sharing roles and responsibilities, and my dearest, a modern man, agreed to cook a meal once a week. But it became pretty obvious early on that if we relied on him to prepare, or even just arrange the meal on the Wednesday evening (a day he decided on for himself) we would go to bed hungry. In more than 21 years of marriage, he has never cooked a single meal from scratch. I have made my peace with this. I am definitely the better cook – it's easy to be better than someone who does not cook at all!

What Zain lacks in culinary skills, though, he more than makes up for in other ways. He is the most responsible, caring, attentive and supportive husband and father. He does more than his fair share of everything else – including cleaning, laundry, shopping, and, when we moved out of a flat into our house, all of the gardening as well. There is a great deal of mutual respect and recognition of our contributions to the relationship. We each have our skills and we work at our marriage jointly, every day.

Am I making it sound easy? Don't kid yourself. Marriage is not easy, not by a long shot. I'm not presumptuous, either. What works for one couple may not for others. Find something that you are both passionate about – then there will always be something to talk about. I have found (the not-so-easy way) that compromise and mutual respect are more important than who is right. It is easier to let the little, and sometimes even the not-so-little, things go. There's no such thing as a perfect marriage, just as there isn't a perfect husband or wife.

Every couple argues; that's a no-brainer. What's important is how one reacts after a fight. The first thing I do is make myself a cup of tea and cut a large piece of whatever cake has been baked and wolf down at least two cookies. A girl's gotta do what a girl's gotta do, right?

Sorry, I've got to run. My husband will be home anytime now, and I've learnt never to keep him waiting for his food.

Some like it hot!
Gouwa Gabier

When a young man tells his family about a girl he has met, some of the first questions that are asked revolve around food.

"Can she cook? Can she bake?"

Naturally the man replies, "Yes!"

His mother asks if he's sure, because she knows how much he likes his good homemade food, and then she proudly says, "I know how fussy you are with your food." She forgets to ask if they share the same goals, values and ambitions. The prospective daughter-in-law's ability to cook and bake is definitely more important than her character and spirituality.

When a young girl has perfected a family recipe, she is praised with compliments, which are often followed by the famous comment, "Now you are ready to get married!" Recreating a family recipe to perfection elicits a silent pat on the back from mother to daughter, reassuring both that the daughter has been raised well and that the mother has done her duty by roping her into kitchen duties from a young age, making sure she pays attention to all the ingredients and steps in the dish. When a bride-to-be can cook, it allows the mother of the bride-to-be to confidently send her daughter into her mother-in-law's kitchen, knowing that her daughter will do her proud and that the groom's family will see that he has chosen well.

However, when a newly-wed bride, eager to please her groom, makes fresh *roti* from scratch and he says, "This is nice honey, but you should ask my mom how she rolls her *roti* because hers is buttery and flaky," then you know that he will spend the night on the couch! I am sure that this happens in every marriage; the groom inadvertently deflates the bride's ego and saps some of her confidence. Let's be honest, we either choose not to ever make *roti* again, or we become so determined to gain his approval that we try to perfect the task. And then, without realising it, the competition between mother-in-law and daughter-in-law has begun, combined with a slight streak of jealousy. And on a Sunday night, when my mother-in-law calls and my dear husband answers the call, and her question, "What did you have for supper tonight?" is answered honestly with either "I heated Friday's left over pizza" or "I made myself some two-minute noodles", then I feel like taking the phone from him and hitting him over the head with the imaginary roast leg of lamb that he should have answered with, instead!

Let's not forget the other famous quote: "The best way to a man's heart is through his stomach." Feed and delight him with all the delicious heart-warming dishes that fill his belly and soul so much, that all that love spills over into your marriage (provided the oils haven't spilled onto the hot element on the stove, and set off the smoke detector). As they say, "A happy heart equals a happy home."

Food requires compromise in marriage. When the young married couple takes their first trip to the grocery store, it all starts out light-hearted and fluffy until you walk down the shopping aisle and you both reach for a bottle of tomato sauce...one selects All Gold and the other chooses Heinz! Each one's preferred selection brings back personal thoughts of home, good old times and familiarity. This illustrates one of many times when food choices in marriage can become tricky. His choice, her choice, new choice...no joy or 'All Joy'?

The first *Ramadaan* together as a newlywed couple is always memorable; such as having to buy an additional chest-freezer to store all of your mother-in-law's home-made savouries and sauces so that *iftaar* is just the way her son likes it. There are also heart-warming moments, like staring across the table lovingly at each other for *suhoor* (albeit half-asleep) or waking the over-sleeping partner five minutes before time is up, so that he or she can quickly gulp down something for the day.

Food nourishes us physically and emotionally in marriage. Food is often the focal point in our celebrations and accomplishments. Over time, a couple's favourite restaurant will become the one that has a sentimental memory attached to it, from when they first met or went out for a meal (supervised or not). We indulge with food, we celebrate with food, we talk about it, and we taste it and devour every last bite together. Food forces us to be present and connected in our marriages.

We need to love our food in the same manner that we need to love each other: freshly made with the best possible ingredients and consumed with all our senses. Food is often a way to express love for our marriage partner: I cook his favourite foods, and, in return, on Mother's Day he brings me breakfast in bed as a token of his love and appreciation for me.

But let us also acknowledge, respect and appreciate our different attitudes towards food in our marriages. After a lifetime of Lemon & Herb, you are not going to choose Extra Hot, but you will always be pleasantly surprised when he orders Mild so that he can share with you. Eventually, you will get to know each other's preferences so well that you will be able to place meal orders for each other at restaurants, without even having to ask what your spouse would like to eat. But don't expect him to appreciate the ginger and garlic smell of the *biryani,* which he has never enjoyed, when you pop over to check on how the editing of your short story is going!

On a closing note, I am reminded of the story of our Prophet Muhammad (PBUH) who drank from the same cup his wife used, placing his lips on the same place that hers were after she sipped, so as to bring them closer. Let our love for food bring goodness and love for each other, so that our recipe is always successful; rather than letting conflict over food cause our marriages to boil over or our relationships to be raw or overcooked.

The 'love story' kitchen
Quraisha Dawood

I have always loved cooking...up stories in my head. Growing up as an only child, I often lost myself in books, either escaping into some new world, or creating my own. I mixed words together, watching them dance on paper to create vibrant or funny characters. Only now do I realise the similarities between concocting tales that free the mind and serving a simmering cauldron of *haleem* to warm the heart.

My mother makes a mean *akhni*, a prawn curry that rivals the best in town, and I still refer to her handwritten *khuri kitchri* recipe that sits at the front of my recipe shelf. Once, when my husband-to-be visited, she served *haleem*, and his response was, 'Q, please tell me you know how to make this!' During my school holidays, sometimes spent at my aunt's house, I rolled out the odd square *roti*, helped fill *samoosas* and peeled potatoes for delicious curries. My single-parent mom, however, made it clear that my main job was to do my best at school and university, while she worked and cooked (and cleaned, and did all the other things moms do). I still often burn my kebabs on the stove, thanks to a new, exciting novel (the best thing I ever spent my Clicks cashback points on was a kitchen timer!).

During my engagement, I did take on more responsibility in the kitchen, but between planning for the wedding and getting a new job, cooking was not my first priority. After the wedding buzz and a honeymoon in the Drakensberg, I was brought to earth by the reality that I would have to cook for a man (who eats steak! And mushrooms! And butter chicken!).

Alone in the kitchen, my tongue was not used to the word 'wife'; my fingers were used to the slim pages of a book, not a ladle; and my eyes were trained to look for bestsellers, not to know when the onions were brown enough. So I just made what I knew. The first day my husband returned from work, I made him (drum roll) *aloo* fry and grilled chicken (ta-daa!). He ate it happily and I was just proud that everything tasted like it should have. Allah has blessed me; my husband is not one to complain.

In my family, we are not big eaters of rich foods, like steak done in butter, and adventurous things, like mushrooms (unless it's on pizza). Armed with my copy of "Indian Delights" and after an intense Googling session, I decided to try making butter chicken. In the end, I called on my kitchen whisperer friend, Arifa, who gave me a fool-proof recipe. The result was delicious and full of flavour, and I swear I have never seen my husband wordlessly light up like that.

Just like writing, once you get the confidence to try, you venture into new territories – that territory being steak (or, as my mom calls it, with a crinkled nose, *ghai jo ghos* – hard meat). Enter "Indian Delights". I made a steak curry, which filled my new home with aromas of tomato and spices and was a feast for the eyes as the robot peppers simmered happily next to each other. Sadly, the result wasn't all happiness and rainbows – the steak itself was overdone and hard enough to break a window. We ate around it.

In time, I have learnt what works for me and how to season and check for doneness. On my journey, there have been numerous burnt pots of rice, flopped cakes, and once I even burnt ready-made *puri patha* (yes, it is possible). Through all this, my husband patiently praised and ate happily, and now and then we got into the kitchen together, making pasta; and once we even made a six-layered rainbow cake! My writing seemed to draw inspiration from these aromas and new successes in the kitchen, and this led to the start of a personal recipe book. Eventually, flavours just came naturally. There were and still are things I hate doing. I can't stand the feeling of raw mince and I have sworn never to make kebabs. Somehow, though, when you cook for a special person, the unpleasant practicalities pale in comparison with cooking's power to allow one to express one's love.

In this day and age, though, I admit that this expression of love must go both ways. Between running my business, keeping up with my three-year-old son and doing errands, cooking does sometimes seem like a chore. On those days, I find it is important to communicate with my husband and come up with a dinner plan. Whether he cooks, we have take-out or we just pop something in the oven to grill, the important thing is that we eat together at the end of the day.

Food is a huge unifier. It is there in times of celebration and sadness. It brings us together in the kitchen or around the breakfast table on a Sunday morning. Food turns a beach day into a picnic. It is the thread that binds me to my culture and my religion. For me, it is a way to express my love to those around me, especially my husband, who works extremely hard to provide for us. When my mom sits down at my dinner table, it is a way for me to thank her for letting me pursue my dreams, rather than making cooking a chore. For my son, it's a way of showing him that mom will always bring him comfort. On days when I don't have to cook and my family cooks for me, it is their way of caring for me (and giving me peace of mind that they would survive if I got sick).

I am still learning how to cook steak properly, but I do feel confident when I walk into the kitchen. Just like writing a love story, the characters are lined up, waiting to cross paths in a delicious plot twist. On some days, they will happily surprise each other; on others they will crave predictability or even not be compatible. (Do not add cinnamon to chicken tortilla. Ever). The secret is to make food memorable. The next time you see a lady in the kitchen, don't think she is 'just cooking'. No, she is writing a story that will nourish her family and long be remembered.

If food be the music of love, play on...
Zayboon Motala

In 1976, I moved to Brazil, and on a fateful evening six months after I had arrived, I met with a car accident which left me physically disabled. For eleven long years I could not walk and for the nine months that a cast was wrapped around my body, I needed to be assisted in every way possible. Before the accident, I had failed to take notice of the needs of physically challenged people. The accident opened up a new dimension in my life and allowed me to view my contemporaries in a different light.

In May, 1987, I started walking again. I walked with a severe limp, but that did not deter me from carrying on with achieving my goals in life. My disability did, however, deter me from marriage because men in my community were not very accepting of my disability. Although I had received many marriage proposals, I had refused all of them. I knew what I wanted and needed in my life. I had given marriage much thought and I knew that I did not want to be pitied by my husband-to-be.

At the age of 60, after years of disability and self-growth, I finally had the courage to embark on a new chapter of life. I remember receiving a call from a friend, asking if I'd be interested in meeting someone. That rainy day, when I walked through the door with a tray laden with fruit, was the beginning of my blissful relationship with Mohammed Areington.

Six weeks after Mohammed had proposed, we made *nikah*. I was a new bride and I now had new responsibility. The number one priority was food. Fortunately, I could cook, but I was faced with every new bride's dilemma – what should I cook? What would my husband enjoy? These questions faced me daily.

I soon realised that it is much easier having a weekly cooking plan. After all, it's not that difficult, once you know what dishes you both fancy. It is also important to have your spices, ingredients, vegetables and meat on hand. I drew up a grocery list on a monthly basis and I spent only within my means.

Not long into our marriage, I came home from the school where I taught to a surprise. Mohammed greeted me with a face full of warmth and love.

"You really deserve this," he said. Mohammed had prepared a sumptuous fish dish with pasta. I was truly taken by surprise. That day, he confessed that his late wife had been asthmatic and was allergic to the smell of oil, and therefore at times he used to take it upon himself to cook for the family. I, too, cooked many of his favourite dishes and sometimes we cooked together. Food at these times became the music of our love. The character of our kitchen transformed to a space of shared responsibility when we cooked together. *Alhamdullilah*, we had a beautiful understanding when it came to matters of cuisine.

Our time together was to span only five years. Mohammed's passing away left me with a treasured but short-lived marriage. I realised that the bond of marriage is very different to every other; whether one is married for a month, a year or fifty years, losing a partner is one of the hardest experiences to accept.

Even though I did not have any of my own children, years ago I had adopted Julia Nomsa Sihlongonyane (Zuleikha). Zuleikha's mother, Emily, who had passed away, had worked for my sister Zuleikha Motala Sayanvala. Two days before Emily's death, she had left her three children in my sister's care, and had asked her to raise them as Muslims. My sister, being the philanthropist she was, had gladly taken these children under her wing. My daughter, Julie, as I fondly call her, also lost her father when she was six years old. When I met my dear Julie for the first time, I could see the sadness in her eyes and I made *duah* to Allah to help me remove her pain. Today she is a confident young *aalima* and has recently gotten married. I am now a mother-in-law and a new chapter in my life has begun.

My advice to Julie and to other young brides is:

Special moments are captured when we drop the rush, hustle and bustle and make time to sit back and enjoy meal times together. Food not only affects our body but also our mind. Tastes, textures and aromas add spice to food. You can purchase recipe books, but remember that, if your food is not tasty, there is no need to grouse and get upset. Try and give it your best shot and you will get it right the second time round. Don't give up and say you can't. Remember, practice makes perfect. Be patient and give yourself time. Buying 'take-outs' is not the way to go, as these meals are expensive and unhealthy. Always remember that the rich aroma of your freshly made curry that welcomes your husband home after a long day at work will not only warm his stomach but also his love for you.

The Prophet Muhammed (PBUH) said that when a husband and wife look at each other with love, Allah the Almighty looks at them with mercy.

Pearls of wisdom

My advice is to stay near your mum if you're challenged in the cooking department; or, if you can, why not support the home industries? **Khalida Moosa**

A tin of baked beans, prepared by either spouse, with a loving hand and served with pride always tastes better than a resentful pot of biryani. **Razina Theba**

Food is food – irrespective of whether it's bought or homemade, whether you made it or your husband did. Eating together is what's important. **Afzad-Al**

Eat together and without the distractions of a TV or the like. Breaking bread together is a time to share and learn about each other. **Raashida Khan**

Don't let cooking take over your life and don't let the kitchen enslave you. **Somayya Hansrod**

Why is food such a big deal? I really wish it wasn't! Hopefully, your husband can cook a little, too... **Aneesa Bodiat-Sujee**

Be clear about your likes and dislikes, otherwise you'll suffer in silence (like I did)! Make your own dishes, while accommodating your husband's tastes, as well.
Maymoonah Chohan

HARDSHIP AND CONFLICT
∙∙∙∙∙∙∙∙∙∙∙∙∙∙∙∙∙∙∙∙∙∙∙∙∙∙∙∙∙∙∙∙∙∙∙∙∙∙∙

He rang me one day, confessing his love for me and promising happiness for life. The conversation lasted for half an hour and his mature tone was convincing enough for me to believe him and his promises. The persuasions felt like assurances to me, and the determination in his tone made me feel emotionally safe with him. Immature and innocent as I was, I believed him; I was convinced that he was the ONE, and was overwhelmed with excitement. Both the families met and the dates were fixed. The wedding finally over, I was on cloud nine. I felt like the most beautiful person on Earth. How was I to know the misery that lay ahead?

Shauqeen Mizaj

My Bollywood movie love
Yumna Samaria

Ours was a love story of the worst kind! We were neighbours as children and I could not stand the sight of him as a teenager. He pursued me relentlessly, until the inevitable Bollywood movie plot started playing out. I fell hopelessly, madly in love, and no warning from family and friends could save me from the turmoil I found myself in. All other suitors were no longer an option. They came, I treated them unfairly, and they left. Somebody should have started SPCS – Society for The Prevention of Cruelty to Suitors. The doors of possibility were now closed and the menus taken away, for I knew what I wanted and had already ordered.

There was now only one man for me, but my family were totally against the marriage. Once I had placed my order and found that they would not give in, I changed into that customer every restaurant dreads: I caused a huge commotion, banged the plates, called the manager and refused to pay. I shamed my parents and family in true disobedient-child style. By now I had thrashed my reputation, and bashed the remainder of my integrity. My parents became prisoners of the war I fought – the ransom I demanded was marriage to the man I loved.

Eventually, my mother succumbed. I was so happy to receive her blessings.

Someone had spoken to someone who had spoken to someone who had spoken to him – my father. Everybody feared my father, and when requests had to be made, they would pass the buck on, saying: "No, you ask him," "No, you ask him," and this trend carried on, until at last he heard through the grapevine.

Eventually...the boy's side found themselves in our home eating Aunty Minim's pineapple sour cream dessert and Aunty Fowzie's star-shaped crème caramels in red-stemmed dessert bowls. I wore the dress my mother forced me to wear and I served my future granny-in-law like a gracious lady (as we had been taught). According to mother and him, serving graciously is one of the greatest impressions you can present to your guests. When you serve, always smile. When you smile, bend your back (upright serving is a rejection of the guest and/or their intentions).

The wedding house

Preparations for the wedding went full steam ahead. Menus were planned, re-planned and abandoned, and anything was made. Clothes were bought and returned, and brothers were sent to re-buy the returned clothes.

Chotikhalas and all kinds of *khalas* were 'called' (informed)... *fooi*'s did not need to be called – they called us! London to Laudium, America to Azaadville, India to Isipingo – everybody had to be called. At the wedding house, anyone could use the phone at no cost, at any time, all the time. The front door never closed, the car never had any petrol, and children had to sleep anywhere because the *khalas* took their rooms. Mattresses were stored under the sofas. No one knew for sure where anyone else was – "I think he went to fetch the *naankata*". Young men who could drive became errand boys. *Achaars* were made, *chevro* was mixed, and *samoosas* were filled – tea served before filling and tea served after filling.

Picture this...Aunty Ayesha and Fatima Dadoo are always making tea, which is a prestigious job at a wedding house. Everybody's domestic workers come to help: they arrive dolled up to wash the dishes, while the *khalas* arrive in their aprons, looking like domestic workers. As soon as the fresh chickens are delivered, to be slaughtered and washed for the wedding meals, the young single girls disappear. Strangely enough, they all re-appear at supper time, dressed to kill (pun intended) and starving.

This was the wedding house: buzzing with excitement and preparation.

I regarded our love as steadfast as a granite fort. All cautionary advice fell on deaf ears.

"Agh, what do they know, they were never really in love," I thought. "That will never happen to us!"

They all reminded me: "You are not marrying the man only, you are marrying his entire family."

And I replied nonchalantly, "Oh? What happened to you is your *indaba* – let's see them try to put their names on our *nikah* certificate!"

With the *nikah* certificate in hand

And so, with the *nikah* certificate (our names only) we began the rest of our lives. For the reception, my father and his cousins (all renowned cooks) outdid themselves. The food and my eligible, handsome brothers were all everyone could talk about, and to us Indian Muslims that level of praise equates a successful reception.

Before we knew it, we were off to the first night. I was eager to see what the hype was about. All my recently married friends and cousins had bragged that the nuptial night was "Bew-ri-full, just bew-ri-full!" For me, on my first married night there was nothing 'BEW-RIFULL' about sitting semi-clothed in scraps of fabric worth a semester's university fees, quivering and waiting, waiting and shaking – sniffing at my underarms. Why hadn't someone, anyone, given us Calmettes an hour before? (Since no one had any mercy on us, I now take it upon myself to instruct flowered girls on the basic flight plan regarding first nights. What you require is more than just your safety belt for turbulence. Take the tablets. You also need your gas mask for cabin pressure, and, of course, the rubber dingy for an ocean landing, with your wash rag and towel to dry you after.)

Days passed as they always do. The *mendhi* on my hands faded away, leaving space for me to creatively jot down recipes. I couldn't cook and needed to keep my secret hidden from my in-laws.

'Make *vagaar*'...pretend that I have an itch, scratch, lift my sleeve, read...'Braise meat until halfway cooked'...Make small talk with my in-laws, braise, 'itch', read, scratch, read, 'itch', read until the dish is cooked and my arms are red and raw.

Within a few years into marriage, we were riding the carousel of life together, dizzy and wanting to get off, wanting to enjoy more, realising that only the Hand of our Creator had the power to flick the switch. We didn't know how long the ride would be, how fast, how slow, how many people on it, when it would it stop. We only rode.

Every marriage has its ups and downs

When I look back now, I see a hazy picture of blue-skied, turbulent times, characteristic of all new marriages. Every newly married woman naively thinks that they are the very first victim, but history repeats troubles with no solutions, and deep sadness with no cures. In my life, these were not confined to my marriage only; they were part of the whole story that had been written already for me. New life, death, disappointments, resentments, abuse, betrayals, exquisite rapture; a new tear to old problems. All this, amidst splashes of love growing in hues of intensity. Love in every colour – angry love, compassionate love, shy love, fierce love, sunny love and, of course, rainy love.

My advice to others

My story is far from over, but, for now, this is my advice to those who enthusiastically attempt marriage.

a. Before the *nikah*, the couple needs to consult a qualified counsellor, who will advise them and help them through their marriage decisions.

b. Both spouses need to have Islamic knowledge of finances, and they need to know the importance of accountability – not only to their spouse, but ultimately to their Creator as well. Beware of the problems related to credit cards! "Petrol! On *udhaar*?" my father exclaimed when I swiped my credit card at the petrol station. He advised me to always live within my means. Read *surah* al Waqiah*, he advised, as this will sustain your household; you will never go hungry, nor will you have to borrow or accept financial aid.

c. Do not focus on being a culinary goddess; rather learn how to prepare two full course meals and one dessert to safeguard your reputation. It is sad but true that we tend to judge new brides when they cannot cook – this ill judgement may result in harsh repercussions within the marriage.

---

* The Prophet (PBUH) said, 'Whoever recites surah al Waqiah at night would never encounter poverty' (Ibn Sunni 620). The Prophet (PBUH) said, 'Surah al Waqiah is the surah of Wealth, so recite it and teach it to your children' (Ibn Asakir).

From point A to point B; beyond ocean and continent
Najma Ansari

I married late in life. At the time, I was working and living in Europe, where I had grown up and received an education. I left my whole life there, to marry an educated, decent, good-looking guy from the developing world. I moved, lock, stock and barrel, from point A to point B – beyond ocean and continent.

I had many expectations, even though the best pre-marriage advice I received from a younger cousin was, "*Baji*, have no expectations!"

Later, I would regret not taking that advice.

When you marry late, supposedly you are well aware of the choices you make. I am so glad that a friend asked me, prior to marriage: "Are you marrying for the sake of marriage, or is this the man you want to marry?"

I'm grateful I had a chance to think it through... It took me a minute or two, as I tried to unscramble my thoughts about which it was, until I was able to say proudly that this was the man that I wanted to marry.

Living in a developing world, spending days with no electricity and water, enduring the countless mosquitoes and melting in the intense heat often got me down, and many times I wanted to throw in the towel. But I recognised that the choice had been all mine. I could blame no one; I had to take ownership of my life.

Alhamdulillah, after nearly 30 years of marriage, I can say that my relationship eventually got better and better, and life is now one long honeymoon – albeit of a different kind.

What helps?

a. Know what you want. I wanted an educated spouse with a good profession from a decent family. Going to a developing country wasn't something I had anticipated, however, I was confident that my core values would see me through. My key advice: don't go for outer trappings. Look for core things you can't do without. Water, electricity and a telephone comfortably qualify as basics, but I compromised on them. I could not compromise on education and basic family decency.

b. Know that you are often the cause of your own grief. I would scramble through a crisis and look for the way in which I was responsible, however miniscule. Knowing how I influenced the problem always served to calm tempers.

To start with, I struggled with communication in my marriage. I wanted to see life through my husband's eyes. How does an expressive wife deal with a spouse who doesn't share his office world? I was insulted and believed that my husband didn't think me worthy. I realised later that my husband had grown up believing that work matters should not be shared. A great deal of grief caused, not just to myself, but to my spouse too, was because of my perceptions and, of course, my unfair expectations.

I failed to see the gems that littered my way, because I was looking elsewhere. When I didn't get flowers on my birthday I decided my husband didn't love me. The fact that I got a much needed fridge on my anniversary escaped my notice.

The most wonderful learning curve is realising that we grow up on what the media dishes out to us, rather than appreciating things that matter and what it means to be loved. I have had to learn to see the gems in my married life.

c. Foster adaptability and imagination, and hang on for dear life. I'm so grateful for my home-grown religious upbringing. My father's key words of wisdom to me were, "Don't be a slave to habits." I adopted his advice and chose only to have my *salaah* as a constant in my life. Tea and then...no tea! Water and then...no water. I got on with life. I accepted what was dished out and adapted to every new situation. A dinner in darkness became a five-star candle-lit meal.

d. Value *salaah* and the Quran. The value of two *nafl salaah* became my magic potion. I bowed down before my creator when going to in-laws, before an interview, for my son's first day of school – before doing anything that I felt anxious about. I found a *salaah* break when the lights went out in the middle of cooking supper. Darkness does not prevent anybody from prayer. A lack of water will make ablution difficult, but, when using my last jug of saved water, I found that the water supply always returned. Miracles do happen if you channel your energies in that direction. And yet, moments of frustration are always waiting to burst. Reading the Quran gives me my daily dose of energy.

e. Education helps. It gives you an edge and helps you to recognise things as they are. I was able to take the leap into a different world, believing that one day my educated husband would be able to join the world I grew up in. It took me a decade to realise that my hope was my dream only, and yet another decade to adjust to my new life, but – it has been well worth the wait.

Seek your husband's advice
Khairun-Nisaa Dadipatel

Whenever a cousin or friend gets married, we have those days, just before the wedding, when everyone sits around and gives advice to the bride-to-be. More often than not, this turns into a fully-fledged ordeal of teasing. At this point, not only the bride becomes shy; some of us married women also start going into shy mode.

Anyway, when it comes to giving advice, I tell this to every single bride out there: the most important thing in a marriage is to make *mashwera* with your husband about everything. If your husband is not happy about a decision that you are undertaking – honestly – do not go through with it. Because, believe me, it will backfire so hard back at you, you won't even know how it happened.

My story is a simple, yet educational, anecdote. I married in my teens, at an age when I still yearned to experience life*. My pressing desire at the time was to pierce my ears – I already had two holes in each ear and I desperately wanted a third hole, as well as a hole on my upper earlobe. I tried to persuade my husband to grant me permission to pierce my ear lobes again and he grudgingly agreed to the third hole; only, I went ahead and pierced the upper ear lobe as well. My husband did not speak to me for days afterwards.

The third hole healed, but the upper ear lobe piercing became infected. I couldn't touch the ear or sleep on it, as it was throbbing and had started to bleed. I did not complain – my pride kept me in check. Deep down, I knew that, because I had pierced my upper earlobe without the approval of my husband, the pain and infection were my punishment.

Months later, I decided to remove the earring, only to find out that the ear would need to be operated on, because cartilage had grown around the earring. I could have the earring removed, but it might not heal properly. So, instead I have left it. Living with this scar reminds me that I should have taken my husband's advice.

* Sadly Khairun-Nisaa Dadipatel lost her husband shortly after this story was written.

At a time when marriage meant everything
Sabera Chothia

I would like to share my mother's story with you because the strength of her marriage to my father was almost heart-breaking, at a time when marriage meant everything.

My mother, Saaleha Jina, was the youngest of seven children. She was born to Fatima and Ahmed Jina on a chilly morning in Carolina, a small town between Ermelo and Barberton, in the year 1950. She was a bubbly child by nature; the playmate of her older siblings.

At the tender age of fourteen – an age when most young girls are only just finding out about love and developing a crush on the boy next door – my mother married my father, Mohammed Ebrahim Chothia, from Vlakpoort. My father saw my mother at a wedding reception in Standerton, and, on his request, his parents sent the proposal. My mother told me, "In those times, we never used to see each other before the wedding, I only saw him on the stage when he came to put on the ring." My mother was not too happy when she saw my father, but her parents had arranged the marriage and she was confident that they only had her best interests in mind.

My mother was not involved in any wedding preparations; her sister and her cousin's wife prepared everything for her. The reception was held in Carolina at her parents' home. Looking beautiful in a Penny Coelen-style* wedding dress, she sat on a makeshift stage in her parents' home, with four bridesmaids who sat at her sides.

"I sat on a stage, but not thinking that I'm getting married. I only realised when I left my mum, my parents; that's the time that I realised that I was getting married."

My mother moved to Vlakpoort to live with my father and his parents. Vlakpoort in those days had no neighbourhood of houses. On a gravel road, in the centre of a black township, there were two prefabricated houses, a shop and a filling station. This was where my mother spent her married life. My father and his parents ran a huge general dealer store, selling goods to the surrounding rural townships. My mother went daily to the shop to assist.

Before the wedding her aunt had told her, "See, you have only two pairs of parents, that is, your father-in-law and your father, mother-in-law and your mother. Whatever your mother-in-law tells you, you must listen, because she as a mother is telling you."

My mother always told me, "It was not easy to be a young bride. It was not easy for me, a young girl, to go to another house. I didn't understand anything, I was a small child, but anyhow, Allah gave me courage to carry on."

Initially, she had "ups and downs" living with her in-laws. "Difficulties, you know, you have that up and down with your in-laws. But my mother-in-law taught me how to cook and after three years I had a baby, my eldest son and then we got on very well. There were no more ups and downs, you know."

When my mother had perfected the skill of cooking, her mother-in-law handed over the responsibility of cooking to her.

At the age of 17, while she was pregnant with my elder brother, my mother fell. It was the first of several falls, which increased in number after 1985: while on holiday in Cape Town, she fell while using the Eastern toilet. From then on, she fell more often.

Eventually, after many biopsies, my mother was diagnosed with muscular dystrophy, which causes progressive weakness and loss of muscle mass. Knowing how her brother suffered with the disease, my mother struggled to accept the diagnosis. My father became my mother's strength.

"Your father said that Allah is great, and he kept encouraging me. My sickness didn't affect him. And my in-laws also just took it as it came," she told me.

Over the years my mother's muscles became weaker and eventually she became bedridden. She did not want to be a burden to my father and his parents, and she offered to move in with my sister. I remember the day that my mother told my father to take another wife. My father's response was, "How can I get married when you got sick in my house? How can I take another wife?" This showed how strong and selfless my parents' love for each other had grown.

Mother said: "Your father used to feed me, bring food for me…He used to help me here and there. When he passed away, I remembered him mostly at night. At night, he used to bring fruit or something and feed it to me. The night before he passed away, that Sunday night, he fed me with ice-cream. We spoke a lot, not in front of everybody but in the room. Not about the business; I didn't ask him and he didn't tell me, also. We discussed everything else."

Before I got married, my mother's advice to me was, "When your husband is angry, you must overlook it and make *dhikr*. You speak, he speaks and then it becomes a big fight. So, just keep quiet, or walk away and keep on doing your work." On the eve of my *nikah*, my mother told me that I was going to a new home and must always keep her *izzat*.

My mother passed away on 5 April 2017, at the age of 67. Muscular dystrophy had stolen thirty good years of her life. Her sudden passing is still a shock. I knew that she did not have much time to live because the muscles around her lungs were weakening, but I had always thought that, because of her inner strength and resilience, she would stay with me for many years to come. Allah's love for her was greater. My mother had always prayed for a quick and easy death and her prayer was accepted.

My mother had patience in everything that she endured in her life. She was always highly spirited and positive. She always made *shukr* for everything in her life. Her passing has left me with valuable life lessons: I, too, have learnt to always be positive and to make *sabr*, no matter the calamity or trial. I have learnt to be respectful of my in-laws and to treat everybody with kindness.

My parents were committed to each other and held the sanctity of marriage in high esteem. They taught me that hardship and sacrifices – if lived through together – can bring a couple closer together. My parents stayed together through thick and thin, until death pulled them apart.

---

* Anne Coelen, a South African actress, model and beauty queen, was crowned as the first South African Miss World in 1958.

Reflections of a daughter
Sumayya Mehtar

Throughout history there have been epic love stories, like those of Shah Jahan and Mumtaz, Laila and Majnun, Samson and Delilah and many more. Whilst every woman yearns to experience fairy-tale love, my parents' relationship was nothing out of a romantic story book. My mother got married within the family to her first cousin. *Daadi* was very fond of her niece (my mother), and, hence, before she passed away almost 40 years ago, she insisted that my mother marry my father, her youngest son and the apple of her eye.

To begin with, my mother kept refusing my father's marriage proposal. She had grown up in a liberal home, while my father hailed from a very conservative Muslim background. Eventually, due to pressure from family members, my mother accepted my father's proposal. It was the right decision: despite their differences in upbringing, my parents' marriage has stood the test of time.

My parents got married in a beautiful, intimate ceremony in Sandton, and, without meaning to sound biased, my mother was the epitome of a radiant bride. She still laughs about her disastrous experience at the hair dresser on the morning of her wedding, and how she was driven to the hall in a car with a broken front passenger seat.

My parents worked together to build their marriage. My father became the breadwinner and my mother took over the household chores. She also worked part-time at the bank where her sisters worked, and she did beading and embroidering on clothing for women in the neighbourhood. My mother has always contributed to the household expenses and tried to maintain her financial independence. Until recently, she ran a successful confectionary business from home.

Growing up with my parents, I have learnt that maintaining a successful marriage entails hard work. It encompasses a delicate mix of tolerance, love, compromise, patience and understanding. When my parents got married, it was a lifelong commitment, and, no matter the circumstances, they made their union work. Today, many homes are breaking up, even when couples reside separately from their in-laws.

My mother did not live with her in-laws. After making *nikah*, my parents moved to Azaadville, a small, predominantly Indian suburb that came about due to the Group Areas Act in apartheid South Africa. My father's elder brother and his wife were staying in a council* house, as they were waiting for the completion of their home. My parents moved in with them, and, of course, once my uncle and his wife moved out, they had the whole house to themselves. My mother lived well with her sister-in-law. My mother believes that the ultimate act of maturity is walking away from conflict. If anybody is mean to her, she overlooks it.

I cannot understand the concept of a woman having to pack up and leave her parents' home to live with strangers. I am so attached to my own home that I often joke with my parents that I wouldn't mind marrying a man who would move in with us. He would also need to be an orphan and a good cook: then I would have no in-laws to deal with, and cooking is definitely not my forte. Wishful thinking, I know, but life is full of surprises.

When my mother got married, she did not own a car, and she walked everywhere to get her errands done. In time and with perseverance, she obtained her driver's licence. There was still one problem, though; we only had one vehicle, and my father used it to get to work every day. Eventually, my father bought my mother an old, powder-blue Peugeot 504 – we could always spot her coming down the road from miles away. On many occasions she was teased because of the car she drove. It never bothered her in the least, and neither did it bother my brother and me. We were happy that at least we had a vehicle to get us to school and we no longer had to walk.

When a couple start out their lives together from scratch, they appreciate every small progress in life as a step towards greater successes. We lived in a small council home for ten years. With hard work, my father built us a bigger house. I will never forget the excitement we all felt the day we moved into our new home. Over a period of time, my parents furnished each room to their satisfaction. Getting to where my parents are today did not happen overnight. Building their marriage was a gradual process, which they worked on together.

Today I find that many newly married couples expect to have a fully furnished home, car and even a freezer filled with *masalas* and savouries. If everything is given to the couple at the snap of a finger, what is left to work hard towards? Many couples today have a sense of entitlement, coupled with a total lack of appreciation. When materialism overtakes character and values, it becomes harder to maintain a successful marriage – or any relationship, for that matter.

If Allah has ordained for me a knight in shining armour, I will undoubtedly take inspiration and life lessons from my parents' marital relationship. Their example has shown me that, while no marriage is all smooth sailing, success in marriage can be measured by growing old together, waking up one fine morning and telling each other: "We made it!"

---

* A council house is a small house with basic amenities built by the municipality of the town.

Braving conflict and hardship with perseverance

Anonymous

To most of us, marriage is a glorified event, one we plan for passionately as little girls, perfecting this dream as we grow. Eventually, we reach the special day when we walk gracefully down the aisle, bursting with emotion. As the function ends and the sun sets on the thrill and excitement, a dawn breaks to reveal a side of marriage that we didn't plan for, discuss or expect: the reality of spending every day for the rest of our lives with a new person, in a new home, with a new family and, for some, in a completely new society. This was my reality a decade ago, when I traded my life as a carefree, independent, city girl from a small, loving family for a new life in a small town hundreds of kilometres away from my perfect world, my home.

After my glamorous wedding and tearful goodbyes to my friends, family and just about everyone from our small community, my parents escorted me to my new home. I clearly recall the hollowness in my tummy as I watched their car leave the driveway. This was the last image I had of the perfect world I had left behind.

Moving in and settling down was fairly easy. I had to live with my in-laws, who tried to be polite and helpful. With independence comes bills; so I had secured employment prior to my relocation and began working soon after my arrival. My life was a combination of being a wife, daughter-in-law and an unknown person in a town I knew nothing about. Slowly, the routine of my new life began to take shape, but at the same time a pattern of behaviour started developing in my home that was no longer polite and comfortable.

The winds of change had begun to blow. Subtle breezes at first, they suddenly picked up momentum until they became a tornado so powerful, I could barely keep anchored at times. The conflict that was brewing broke down my independence, and people who sought to have a sense of power over me attempted to reduce me to a point where my very identity and existence were controlled.

It started with me not being allowed to receive calls from my parents, friends and relatives after working hours, and escalated to where I was told my parents were not to visit me unless there was someone present to oversee the visits. The domestic worker was periodically put off; my entertainment was confined to television and food. Communication thrived when the topic involved slandering my parents and siblings. New rules were imposed on me regularly, regarding where I could and could not travel to and whom I could and could not befriend. The nature and level of the conflicts varied, from being verbal exchanges of harsh and patronising words to trivial, non-verbal kinds, like disconnecting the washing machine, keeping all the rooms in the house locked, forcing me to living out of a suitcase and bin bags; all in an attempt to increase the power exerted over me.

At this time, my husband's attitude went from kind and caring to impatient, insulting and angry. He thought nothing of degrading me in full view of his family, or any available audience, for that matter. These scenes dug the foundation for a larger scale of abuse, which escalated after the birth of my first child: physical abuse.

Reflecting on this period, I have learnt to understand why women in abusive marriages cannot simply leave. Facing this kind and level of abuse, after being raised for almost three decades in a home and family where women are respected, loved and honoured was the greatest shock to my existence. I remember feeling pain, guilt, remorse and embarrassment. I clearly remember typing messages to my father and brother and then deleting them, out of fear of what might happen next, guilt about having a broken home, and embarrassment about packing up and returning home. I remember asking myself how my parents would explain my predicament to others and worrying about whether I would be bringing them shame. The few times I got to be with them, I wanted to soak up their faces and smiles and make the most of their company, silently dreading what awaited me when they left.

My world was spinning out of control, with each aspect of my life becoming more unidentifiable. I was unrecognisable to myself, a complete emotional wreck, moving between overwhelming despair, fear and guilt to moments of weak happiness each time I held my firstborn and tried to be the best mother I could be in the circumstances. These moments rekindled my hope and rejuvenated my spirit, even for a short while.

This is the reality of the internal conflict abused women in middle-to-high income society face and largely the reason we remain silent on an issue which begins to kill. I was no exemption. My husband's increasing drug addiction escalated the episodes of slapping and punching, and a few months into the abusive cycle, I was taken to hospital to meet the crushing news of a miscarriage, just days after finding out I was pregnant with my second baby.

Desperate and alone, on a theatre bed waiting to have a dilation and curettage (D&C), I mentally raced through my life and how I had landed here. I thought about my firstborn and how I was failing him daily. I thought about myself and how a once full and complete person was now falling rapidly into an abyss. I was in a cycle that was consuming me and stealing away my child's right to safety and happiness. I realised how much I missed my home, the sound of my father's voice, the comfort of granny's smile and the safety of my mother's eyes. Most of all, I really missed me. Those moments before the anaesthetic disconnected me from my reality were brutal, painful and sobering, all at once.

I left the hospital on a mission to heal myself, to fix what I had broken, and to rise above the internal and external conflict. My baby's death marked the end of a nightmare and the birth of my determination to take back my right to happiness, success and contentment. It was time I shielded my son from any further danger.

I cried my story to any person willing to listen, painfully learning that a listening ear is also a running mouth. I cried out for help to the *jamiat*, whose best advice was to have *sabr*. I continued to battle my ego, which even at this time prevented me from reaching out to my parents. I owed credit facilities enormous amounts of money, because I had started a business that was barely sustainable. I was trying to get a grip on motherhood, which unmasked my incompetence at every opportunity. And I was trying to fight the biggest demon of all, my husband's drug addiction.

For the most part of this time, nothing seemed to have changed despite my efforts, except for a new element that had entered my life: prayer. I had started to pray more often and would find myself begging, pleading and desperately crying out for Allah's help. Time was moving on swiftly and I was now a mother to two children, my eldest not even two years old.

The need to support my children saw me pulling out all the stops to earn enough, and, in all this, Allah's mercy began to rain down on me. What started out as drizzles of mercy eventually became a storm. A beautiful storm – the kind that settles the dust. With Allah's help and mercy, my life slowly started shifting to a positive place. I became self-sufficient. I managed to support and encourage my husband through his battle with drugs. I performed *Umrah*, moved to a new home and gave birth to my third child, all in a short space of time. I went back to university to complete postgraduate degrees. My passion for life was restored, along with the dignity and respect I desperately yearned for. All this was possible through Allah's blessings upon me and my family.

My journey has compelled me to add my voice to the voices of thousands of women who battle abuse daily, with no escape in sight. The lessons from my journey form the base of my message to all women who are enduring hardship and conflict in the context of their relationships.

After hardship comes ease but that ease should never be at the expense of your dignity, your safety and your sanity. My greatest mistake was holding back from seeking the love and support of my family. My weakness was succumbing to the disempowering advice to make *sabr*. The reward for *sabr* is written by Allah, but there is a stark difference between *sabr* in the context of material hardship and *sabr* in the context of oppression, abuse and violence. I advocate strongly against the latter.

The hardship and conflict I endured on my journey detracted me from the journey I had envisioned for myself. However, in retrospect, it was a humbling experience, which taught me empathy and woke me to the reality of struggling for emotional and mental survival.

Ultimately, this journey has shaped my personality positively and taught me the critical skill of picking my battles. Most importantly, it has taught me that *duah* is the most powerful weapon of a believer and no pain is permanent. An important pearl of knowledge I would like to share with all those walking the path of marriage, is to expect the unexpected and maintain a level head, no matter how hard it may seem to be.

We all carry within us the solutions to our problems; although this only becomes apparent to us once we've recognised the lesson we are being taught. I carried Allah in my heart through my dark days and He will always be with me. I pray my journey is a lesson to all those who plan to marry and a means of strength to those who are enduring struggles within their marriage.

If only I had known
Nurnazida Nazri

It was the toughest decision I had to make, especially when I live in a society where it is still considered taboo. People look down on you and give you the pity face if they know about what you are going through. However, deep down in my heart, I knew I had to come to that decision; I really had to take the plunge. I repeatedly consoled myself, "Well, look at it this way. It's just like taking off the plaster from your wound. It will hurt you, but you will feel relief after that." And it was not a lie, either. It was a really hurtful experience and certainly an unforgettable one.

A few months into our marriage, I knew that we were more than half way to hitting rock bottom. We had disagreements about everything and anything. I was not sure what the real reason was behind our conflict, but I could see the hatred that was burning in his eyes.

Both of us agreed on a clean divorce. There, I have said it: the 'D' word, frowned upon by many who look down on anyone holding the status of 'divorcee'. Personally, I would not advise anyone to go through what I did. Yet, if there is nothing left in a marriage except the excitement of constantly trying to hurt one another, then it is the best decision to make.

We tried everything to mend the marriage and divorce was the last resort. I worried about what people would say, but I worried more about my sanity. I tried to imagine living with my husband for another thirty years and I couldn't. That was when I knew I had to take the dreaded action.

It was a lonely, depressing journey. I did not have anyone to share my feelings with. I stayed with an aunt, and, because I did not want to burden her with my problems, I put on a happy face every time I left the room. In all honesty, I was ready to jump in front of a moving car and end my life. Hope seemed to be so far away. I felt like a trapped kitten waiting to be rescued by anyone who actually cared. The worst part was explaining my situation to my colleagues. In the end, I only broke the news to a few close colleagues. I just could not face the embarrassment of the whole office knowing about it.

I am only human, and trying to stay strong and be positive in such a challenging situation was not easy. I cried every night and really took my time relaying my feelings to the Almighty while praying. Of course, looking back at it now, I feel like such a whiner, grumbling about everything that had gone wrong in my life and finger-pointing. If only I had known back then what I know now.

A year after living this trying life, I met a charming man who later became my husband. It was not a fairy-tale romance. We were colleagues and met every day in the office. Fate brought us closer and we decided to tie the knot. He has continued to be my confidante until today, and is a true supporter of whatever decisions I make in life. Sometimes, I take a quick look at him and blush when I remember all my whining, complaining, and feeling of wanting to give up and end everything. Life seemed to be meaningless then and I really wanted it to end.

Being alone taught me valuable lessons. We cannot predict the future. Even during the most trying times in our lives, we should realise that things will eventually improve. All of us are promised different tests in life and all we have to do is have faith in the Almighty. Whenever I am faced with tough situations now, I take a stroll along memory lane, and I feel stronger. I was terribly lonely and depressed after my divorce, but I was given only that which I could handle and I was rewarded soon after for my patience. I now have a wonderful husband, who fell into my life like magic. If only I had known.

When 'the one' is the wrong one!
Shauqeen Mizaj

Marriages are made in heaven, so goes the saying. But marriages are made neither in heaven nor in hell. In fact, it's up to you and your partner to decide whether to make your marriage a heaven or hell.

Just like any normal girl my age, I too dreamt of my Prince Charming, a man who would fall in love with me, and, of course, a happily ever after. I was waiting to see what the Almighty had in store for me. Coming from a well-educated, progressive and financially stable family, where even women went to work, not just to earn a living but also to become self-reliant, I dreamt of having a good life, including a satisfying career. Sounds like a fairy tale?

After school, I enrolled for engineering in a reputable college. During my final year of studies, the so-called marriage talks were in full swing at home. But my world came to a sudden halt when I received a phone call from home. My batchmate at college had met my father and asked for my hand in marriage. My family had completed the conventional practice of inquiring about the groom's family and seemed satisfied. My consent was what they needed.

I was dumbstruck and confused. I wasn't friends with him, and had always thought of him as a spoilt, rich brat, who was poor in studies. I disliked him for being a spendthrift, for his carefree attitude towards life and the people around him. He rang me one day, confessing his love and promising me happiness for life. The conversation lasted for half an hour and his mature tone was convincing enough for me to believe him and his promises. His persuasions felt like assurances and the determination in his tone made me feel emotionally safe. Immature and innocent as I was, I believed him; I was convinced that he was 'the one', and was overwhelmed with excitement. Both families met and the dates were fixed.

After the wedding was finally over, I was on cloud nine. I felt like the most beautiful person on Earth. How was I to anticipate the misery that lay ahead?

The change in my husband's behaviour was drastic. Right from Day 1, he was rude and impatient. He found fault with everything I did: the way I walked, talked and how I dressed. I wasn't allowed to go out without his permission or talk with strangers. He didn't like me using a phone or going to my parents' home. I tried several times to get him to talk about what was wrong. Whatever it was, we could sort it out, I said. But he kept putting blame on me, saying how bad a wife I was, how I didn't respect him and take care of him.

I spent my days in misery. Pursuing my studies or going to work was out of question. Physical intimacy was all that he wanted, often becoming aggressive. My initial attempts to resist him gradually died out. I was reduced to a mere piece of flesh at night; my only purpose was to serve my husband in every way I could. I tried sharing my agony with my in-laws who repudiated my claims. Much to my shock, they advised me to be an obedient wife, take better care of my husband and ignore the pain.

As days passed, my husband continued to rebuke and belittle me in every way he could. At times he was indifferent and cold as ice. He neglected his duties and ignored my presence. Name calling, mockery, threatening with divorce, and criticising my parents for not presenting him with gifts intensified, followed by domestic violence. Marriage had become a nightmare and I was scared.

I hid my agony from my parents, as I didn't want to cause them pain. Years passed, but nothing changed. The pain, loneliness and misery turned into indifference and I retreated into my shell, mechanically engaging in the morning-to-night routine. When my husband went to work, I would sit in my balcony for hours, staring into nothingness, feeling blank and empty. I neither ate nor drank. I had lost my dreams and goals somewhere along the way. I tried hard to remember the kind of person I once was, chirpy, talkative and full of life. I recalled how I loved to laugh, play pranks and crack jokes; I was nicknamed chatterbox at school. Tears rolled down my cheeks when I thought of all those happy moments I shared with my parents and siblings back home.

"Why me?" I asked the Almighty. I prayed to lessen the ache in my heart and to guide me to peace and happiness. I had faith in Him. My life was precious; I couldn't waste it anymore. I couldn't ignore the injustice anymore. I was answerable to the Almighty.

A strange sense of awakening filled me. I waited for two days and called my parents, revealing my misery. They were shattered; but brave enough to bring me home and support me during my tough times. I obtained a divorce, along with a decent alimony, and suddenly, there I was, standing on my own feet: financially independent and enjoying my freedom, living life to its fullest.

It's always better to be alone with dignity than in a marriage that constantly requires you to sacrifice your happiness and self-respect. It's been a year since my divorce, and I am now happily married to a wonderful human being. I am grateful to the Almighty for my husband – the kind of person he is, his unconditional love and the understanding, trust and kindness he displays.

My experiences have taught me that a good marriage requires both spouses to work equally towards strengthening the relationship in ways that benefit not just 'you' or 'me' but 'us'. Marriage is not always about sacrifices and compromises; it's also about working together, hand in hand, comforting and complementing each other, overcoming the big and small hurdles life throws at you. Accept your partners as they are; believe me, they will love and trust you more. Every human being craves to be loved and appreciated. Making genuine efforts, however small, to bring a smile to your partner's face is always worth it.

27 Beautiful lies
Saffiya Ismail Cassim

Truth might be bitter, but its outcome is sweet.
Falsehood appears to be sweet, but it is poisonous in its essence.
Imam Ali (AS)

"Forgive me; I can't cause you any more pain. I said too much and did too little, I love you dearly. It seems there is no amicable resolution with my kids. I have also hurt your son in the process. My kids didn't understand the impact of what they were doing. You are not a failure. Now everyone can see the impact of what they did. I cannot find an amicable solution to bring our families together, better I let go of our *nikah* out of mercy for you, my failure to take care of you, not stand up for you. This is not going to work out. I take responsibility for the failure, I ask for forgiveness a thousand times."

Legs collapsed. Brain stuttered. Lungs heaved. Gut clenched. Anger. My brain barely registered the text message. I scrolled up to read other messages that contradicted this particular one. My hands gripped my phone with urgency, trying to respond, yet the only word screaming in my brain was, "Coward!"

What about the sacred words in the presence of the Almighty, the *Imam*, witnesses? What about all the promises? Anger, more than shock, enough for me to summon the courage to scroll down to his name and dial him. No answer. Almost unintelligible through my tears, my voice shaking, I left a voice message. "Sam, a text *talaq*, really? How merciless?"

I sat there, silent. I clicked the button on my phone, intent on sending a text message. My screen reverted to darkness. I read through all his saved text messages to me; to his final text message. He truly was saying one thing and doing the complete opposite. I needed explanations: why had he married me if he knew everything was not fine on his side? Why the lies and deception? Why had he come along with promises? Why had he not rectified the situation when he had the chance?

I gripped my phone until my fingertips were white from the pressure. I had no one to call; those closest to me were estranged, because of Sam. That message, the death sentence of my marriage, *talaq, talaq, talaq*, had ended all connection I had to my former life, leaving me with tears, broken dreams, shattered hopes, financial ruin and now *iddat*.

When I had embarked on this journey of marriage, I unselfishly gave all of me. I don't think anything I could have done would have changed my collision course.

How it all began...

After returning from an amazing trip to Thailand with my son in 2013, I received a call from my friend's mother. It was one of those talks – a "you should the settle down, we were not meant to be alone" talk. I realised she would not be giving me this talk without an end goal in mind. I was comfortable with my life – it would take someone amazing to change my status – but I agreed to meet Sam over a cup of coffee.

My first words to him were, "Time is precious, I don't want you to waste my time nor will I waste yours, so if your intentions are not clear, please walk away." The "chat" lasted for three hours. He was an introvert, charming, super-intelligent. He had amazing in-depth Islamic knowledge, we shared the same Islamic school of thought, he loved that I was Indian. He exuded the principles I value in a person. We discussed our first marriages; we had both been stranded by fate in circumstances beyond our choosing.

Sam had been divorced for only a year and he was still very angry and bitter. He hated his ex-wife for betraying him and walking out. He mentioned his children were emotionally affected by their divorce. This should have been my red flag.

Unusually, for a composed person like me, Sam swept me off my feet. I threw caution to the wind, and, with a heart full of hope, I took a leap of faith. On 15 September 2013, I married Sam within 99 days of knowing him. His three kids would become mine and my son would become his.

Our new blended family brought excitement, a breath of fresh air for me. We transitioned well initially. I embraced my new role with such hope and eagerness. I planned fun activities when the boys visited, stocked the kitchen, cooked themed dinners, spoilt all with gifts and entertainment. I cannot express how happy I was at that point, blissfully unaware there were deeper issues lurking behind the façade.

Two months after we married, Sam allowed a friend and his family to move onto the property indefinitely. No discussion, I was merely informed. The same month, his older son moved in permanently, whilst his second son started spending most of the time with us. Sam told me they were experiencing problems with their biological mother.

Sam failed to set healthy boundaries within the home. Sharing kitchen, bathrooms, and communal living spaces with his friends became an issue. Nothing was personal or private anymore, not even our own bedroom. Sam would break down constantly when faced with any challenge or if he was questioned about anything. He reminded me of a wounded bird, wanting to soar, but his wings were broken. I became his wings, tried to help him deal with childhood memories that haunted him, and made him react in particular ways.

The tensions between Sam and his ex-wife escalated, due to a legal battle over the house, joint assets and his marriage to me. When my step-children visited her on weekends, they returned angry, and directed their feelings at Sam and me. Eventually, trouble lurked in every corner, ranging from food becoming an issue, to my race being mocked. I found myself in situations I never would have dreamed of. I hate conflict, so most times I looked on, horrified, as I witnessed and experienced things that were out of my control. It was unbelievable how extreme things had become, turning our lives inside out and upside down.

Sam was completely overwhelmed. He would break down, weeping, to my son and me. He was like a pendulum that swung from helpless to unfazed, and back. Deep down, I sensed there was more to this than I knew, but nothing could have prepared me for the truth. The shouting matches between Sam and his children escalated to the point where I found myself being dragged in. I just could not understand where all their anger was stemming from.

My relationship with my son became strained. Rather than watch his mother go through this, my son expressed that he wanted to live on his own. Sam, in a fit of rage, shocked me by saying, "If you move, you must take your mother with you!" My son did not leave; he just drifted further away from me.

The final straw came during one rather ugly scene between his daughter and him. She was a very angry, hurt young lady, who felt rejected and betrayed by her parents, and she became vocal about what she knew. In her anger, she divulged shocking information. I learnt that Sam had lied to me from the very beginning. He actually gave his first wife a *talaq* only in December 2013, months after marrying me. He also lied about being separated a year before; in reality his ex-wife moved out in April 2013. By June 2013, he had started looking for another wife – ME! The children blamed Sam for their mother walking out. They wanted their family back together.

Sam had packaged a gift box beautifully for me, but inside was a volcano. It had erupted.

From that moment, my son and I were subjected to silent treatment. I was in a constant state of anxiety. With friends and family being estranged, I became isolated; Sam's family provided no support and instead added more fuel to the fire, by telling me how to deal with the situation and then denying ever telling me anything.

I admit that, after the daughter's revelations, I intentionally started expecting less and less from the family and marriage, and allowed Sam and my stepchildren to get away with more. I was collateral damage in a war I had not signed up for.

In February 2016, Sam and I mutually agreed that I would move out on my own with my son, because things had deteriorated badly with his children. He said he would find a solution and we would work through all of this. A signed letter of reassurance that he would never *talaq* me sits in my purse as a reminder.

***

When I started this chapter, my fingers slammed the keyboard, my heart ached, and it felt like glass shards were cutting deeply into me. No one has been able to fully understand why I have been so heartbroken over a man who was not the person I thought he was. It's never easy to have to admit failure, when you've given a hundred percent of yourself to a marriage. As I write the closing segment of my chapter, I can tell you that, while the gut-wrenching pain has gone, the memory of it remains.

When Sam gave me a *talaq*, it wasn't just about our marriage ending. It was about the loss of all hope that I shared with him for our future. It was about the loss of time wasted, which I can never get back. It was about the loss of trust. I probably will never know the truth, because it was wrapped in beautiful lies. We think we go in with our eyes wide open.

Divorce is sad and painful, and involves a lot of soul-searching; it really shouldn't be a source of shame, as well. Yet, society still looks at a divorced woman as 'shameful' in words and actions. Sometimes you may not want a divorce, but your partner chooses it as the easy option, instead of doing the right thing.

I think the *iddat* period is a cleanser of grief and anger. When a woman becomes a widow, the pain is unimaginable, but, somehow, there is finality and acceptance that it was decided by our Creator. With divorce, there are always unanswered questions.

I am glad that I went through this process – self-reflection, cleansing and finally forgiveness. I will never see myself as a victim, simply a survivor. I was totally committed to him and 'our' family. Battle-scarred but stronger, I am now re-defining what's important to me – and this doesn't include another marriage. Nothing should ever condone bad behaviour, lies or deception. Condoning this would mean compromising principles in life.

Marriage, to my mind, is supposed to be so permanent, so inviolable. I upheld the sacredness of the *nikah* to the best of my ability. I was the opposite of Sam: I did too much to save us and but said too little about the wrongs.

All I can say now, in the aftermath of Sam, is that he has left me with some of life's lessons. A man with so many inner battles stemming from his childhood, his first marriage, his life in general – I wanted more than anything to help him overcome and heal, but the dynamics were too strong. I believe he never really loved me, he just loved the way I loved him. I pray he doesn't do the same again, that he helps his children, and more importantly, himself, so that history never repeats itself. I see my situation now as having been liberated by my Creator; I was freed from having to fight Sam's battles.

Where am I right now? In my *sujood*, where my most intimate whispers leave my lips, my soul bare to the one who is the master of it. One supplication frees me from all that has transpired.

"O Allah, forgive him. O Allah, forgive his children."

Understanding where conflicts come from

Anonymous

If there is one thing many people never tell you about marriage beforehand, it is that, for some people, it can be one of the greatest trials they will ever personally experience from Allah. Yes, they tell you that you may quarrel here and there, and many counsellors will advise you about how, as a woman, you should avoid or deal with quarrels. But nothing prepares you for a journey filled with so much hardship that you begin to wonder why you went into it in the first place. You look at your spouse and wonder how the person you fell in love with got replaced by someone you hardly know. Every conversation has the potential of turning into a huge fight, and it feels as if your partner doesn't see or acknowledge your position in his life anymore.

While many couples may have arguments and moments of anger, it doesn't degenerate into anything serious. For us, however, marriage has been one of the most trying things we've ever done.

I spent a lot of the early years of my marriage in despair. Nothing was going as I expected and I didn't know how to fix it. "Why aren't we communicating? Why do we fight a lot? Does he hate me, now that we're married?" In my quest to fix whatever was wrong with us, I started searching for the root of the problem, because the chances of permanently resolving any conflict in marriage lie in understanding where it's coming from.

In my search for the source of the problems, I realised two things:

My first realisation was that every one of us has flaws that we need to confront if we are to have a good marriage. Your partner comes into the relationship with personal flaws developed over years, that they may not even realise they have, and that may be toxic to your marriage. On your part, becoming honest about your negative habits could be really important in your quest to eliminate conflict in your marriage. No one is perfect, so when you are counting your spouse's flaws, check yours too, and see how they may be affecting your relationship.

The second realisation is that the solution to our problems may be easier than we thought. For example, many older couples will preach patience and perseverance in the face of conflict in marriage. They may tell you to be calm and say, "That's how all men are". But who would have thought that you could find a solution by speaking out loudly? That by moving from calm to expressive, you would begin to see where all your problems are coming from?

By all means, be patient in the face of conflict. It's is a sign of *hikmah* to calmly understand a problem before reacting, to think twice about your words and actions, so that you do not regret them. But never confuse being patient with being docile. Don't hurt yourself and your marriage by enabling your spouse to hurt you, because you never spoke out against what he is doing wrong. Speak out firmly, but calmly. Have conversations where you expressly say what is on your mind. If he doesn't agree or admit to his mistakes, that is a different ball game entirely, but your issues won't disappear simply because you decided to swallow every hurt.

If I had to pick one thing that worked best as I walked through my trials, it would be prayers. Not just *salaah* and the occasional, "Help me, oh, Allah", but sincere, from-the-bottom-of-your-heart *duah* to Allah. Many people say that prayers work wonders, but you don't appreciate this till it manifests in your life. If you are ever faced with conflicts in your marriage, call Allah by His most beautiful names, seek His help and guidance, and know that He is the only one that can ease your trials.

And as you pray, be prepared to do the legwork. Be prepared to put in the effort that it takes to build a positive marriage. Be ready to change yourself for the better and willing to support your spouse to change too. Be ready to have honest conversations that may not be pretty. Know when to push him to do better and understand when it is best to accept a flaw and live with it. Because, unless you intend to marry someone who is a hundred percent perfect, you can expect your spouse to have habits that you do not care for.

Conflicts happen in marriage, and, like I said earlier, it may be something that Allah has chosen to test you with. But you can make a choice on how you respond to the challenge, so that it brings you and your spouse together and increases your love for one another.

When communication is not enough

Papatia Feauxzar

We often strive to keep the line of communication open in our marriages but it can get to a point where this is not enough. Sometimes the conversation ends with you feeling more perturbed. When this happens, try a different angle and pray to Allah to guide you to do what's best. Some spouses don't like it when you raise something that's been raised before. They'll respond to you as if you are an annoying wood pecker constantly nagging about the same issues. So, it's best to wait until you find a different perspective on how to approach the problem that seems to divide you.

Mostly, we fail to consider our spouse when communicating. You can communicate all you want, but, if you don't take a step back to put yourselves in each other's shoes and try to compromise every once in a while, your relationship will remain stuck. Your demands will fall on deaf ears.

Communication is also pointless if you're a people pleaser. In most relationships, there will be one person who wants to avoid conflicts. Or both spouses will be this way. These days I can get very confrontational, because I now know that avoiding conflict is a 'band-aid' solution, a short-term fix. In the long run, not fighting the good fights will eat at your soul, happiness, and foundation of your relationship. There is only so much you can take before the tipping point!

Always remember that your spouse does not possess a telepathic communication device. (This is my advice to myself.) In fact, half of the time, most spouses don't know what the other is thinking. One minute, spouses can understand each other and the next it's confusion. It's normal. So, when you expect your spouse to read your mind about anything and he or she doesn't, just chill – it's not always about you.

In conclusion, you don't have to be constantly talking or communicating to have a great marriage or relationship. Enjoy the conversation-less moments you share. Silence can also be connection. A lot of spouses don't like talking, but they will meet you half-way every once in a while. And there is certainly something your spouse will expect you to meet him half-way with; that's what compromise is. Just go with the flow.

Marriage and emotional disorders
Layla Abdullah-Poulos

"I think I'm losing my mind." There was no better way for me to express it to my husband. Months of little-to-no sleep and obsessive thoughts keeping me constantly on edge brought me to what felt like the brink of insanity.

The previous year had been a hodgepodge of joy and tragedy that fed the increasingly uncontrollable range of emotions tearing at my insides and exhausting me of any resolve. I vacillated between the happiness of being a new mother of two children and crushing pain at the sudden deaths of my mother and grandmother, at polar ends of what became an indelible year in my life. It also was the year that triggered the worst episode of anxiety I'd ever experienced.

A perfect storm of emotional trauma and post-partum depression exacerbated what I would discover to be generalised anxiety disorder – a condition I have struggled with since I was a child. Back-to-back pregnancies and family deaths left me emotionally raw and unable to cope with my condition. My husband was similarly confounded about what was happening to his wife and the mother of his children.

One frustrating thing about mood disorders is that the sufferer appears fine to everyone around them while symptoms tear at their insides. Save the occasional bad mood, my husband thought I was okay. He slept quietly while my eyes remained wide open and obsessive thoughts about death triggered flight reflexes – heart racing, trembling, hypersensitivity to sound – and I spent the night wide awake. By the time he realised that things were getting worse, I was already deep in my anxiety and trained to parrot the mood disorder refrain, "I'm okay" when I was far from it. *Alhamdulillah*, he didn't buy it. He comforted me and took the lion's share of caring for the kids, while still working.

He made sure all meals were prepared for me and the little ones before leaving for work. He cleaned the house and coaxed his fidgety wife back to bed in the middle of the night. When my anxiety got to the point where I couldn't read Quran, he read it to me, and when I decided I needed professional help, he packed the kids in the car and took me to therapy every week for over a year.

I learnt, after my symptoms subsided, that he had taken the time to get information about my disorder and provide support accordingly. When I told him he was amazing, he thanked Allah for strength and mentioned that he had to be, because his love, wife, and mother of his children needed him to be.

It takes a lot of intuitive, physical, and emotional energy when a spouse is grappling with any illness. Over the past 26 years of marriage, each of us has had to don a cape and tow a heavier line so the other could heal. If we become caught up in ourselves and what we are missing out on because our significant other is ill, we do them a disservice as well as ourselves, as servants of Allah.

Allah says: "And one of His signs is that He created mates for you from yourselves that you may find rest in them, and He put between you love and compassion; most surely there are signs in this for a people who reflect." – (*Surah* 30 Verse 21)

People often think about their spouses and the homes they build together as a respite from the stresses of the world. Additionally, many are prepared to help their spouses with physical ailments conveying obvious illness, but when the spouse's stress emanates from within and the symptoms can be easily dismissed as 'attitude', the ability to provide rest presents a different challenge.

Loving someone with a mood disorder is no different than loving someone without one. There remains the need to understand, value, and respond positively to your spouse's emotional processes. With mood disorders, that may mean becoming astute at understanding how the disorder is affecting the spouse emotionally and physically and responding in a way that doesn't make it worse. It takes patience, kindness, and mercy – which is what we should have for each other, anyway.

Years after one of the worst periods of psychological illness of my life (and may Allah protect me from any more), we both developed skills to recognise when the disorder is presenting. We are also very keen on self-care. I learn to shut out the world when becoming even remotely symptomatic. He understands and will circle the wagons around me so I can heal and become less vulnerable to a downward spiral.

By caring for me while I tackle my mood disorder, my husband is also fulfilling an obligation to Allah as my protector and maintainer. Too frequently, the narrative about marriage is restricted to broad discussions about physical gratification and monetary satisfaction. Rarely is there in-depth discourse about the importance of caring for each other's emotional well-being. There needs to be more of that.

Surviving a traumatic incident: Lessons learnt

Shakira Akabor

On a cold winter's Monday morning, amid the hustle and bustle of getting the kids ready for school, I switched on the air conditioner to warm up our tiled living area. Then I fed our pet African Grey a few naartjie segments, whilst my husband teased him for being unusually quiet. Just before dashing out the door, I considered switching the air conditioner off, but later decided against it, as my little son was playing on the rug. The room will warm up nicely for him, I thought, and called out to my two daughters to hurry up as I went out to start the car. My helper had arrived a short while earlier, and we were ready to go.

The girls got to school ten minutes late that morning. I sighed and thought this was not a good start to my week. Little did I know what was in store. I drove back home, lost in thought. As I waited for the light to turn green, only a minute away from turning into my street, I received a call from my helper. She was sobbing uncontrollably. I called out her name over and over, asking what had happened. A few seconds later, the call ended. Then I began to panic. My son must be in danger, I remember thinking.

Why wasn't she speaking? Horrible thoughts rushed to my head. There must be a robbery! Immediately, I dialled our security company as I turned into my street.

And then I saw it. Huge, billowing black smoke. As if in slow motion, it dawned on me that my house was on fire. In utter shock, I drove past all our neighbours lined up the street watching me as I approached the house. Cars were everywhere. The police. The security company. The ambulance. And there, on the grassy verge stood my helper and my little son. I'll never forget the image of their faces: my darling son's sombre, unsmiling expression and my helper's tear-stained cheeks. Abruptly I stopped the car and ran out to hug them both, crying with relief and thanking Allah that they were fine and unhurt. Just then, I turned to look at the house. Huge, orange flames poured out the lounge window. I started crying. Soon I was sobbing uncontrollably as my helper said our dear parrot did not make it. I watched in utter shock and horror as my beautiful house burnt away, completely helpless to stop the blaze from spreading. I repeatedly asked the police where the fire brigade was. "They're coming, they're on their way," the police reassured me. Twenty minutes later, the firemen arrived with three large red fire engines.

During that time, random strangers offered assistance in any way they could. Tea. Coffee. Hugs. A place to sit. The paramedics rushed over. Did anyone inhale smoke? Did anyone have an injury? Do you need a blanket? Are you okay? I looked at them, bewildered. I couldn't focus or think clearly. All I could think of was that my son was safe and that our dear parrot had just died in the blaze. I shook my head, no. I looked down at my hands that held my son and saw that I was shaking. I just wanted to wait for my husband, I said.

A neighbour held me and took us to her house, whilst my helper recounted the incident: a small fire had started in the lounge air conditioner. My four-year-old son had seen it and alerted her. She had been washing dishes in the kitchen and had not thought much about what he was saying, assuming he was babbling away. But he had come back into the kitchen a few moments later, urgently saying there was a fire in the air conditioner. So she had gone to have a look and saw the flames. She had immediately phoned my husband, who was driving to work at the time.

Before long the fire had spread to the curtains, and, following my husband's instructions, she had taken the boy and run out the house. In thirty minutes, our lounge, dining room, study and kitchen burnt away. As she was talking, I listened intently. Just then, my husband arrived and I fell into his arms, sobbing as he held me. He was calm and quiet. He kept asking if I was okay, was our little son okay? Was the helper okay? I nodded, unable to speak. Soon my sister arrived and helped us pack whatever we could so that we could move in with her. The firemen had deemed our house unliveable. My poor daughters did not know a thing until they got home from school, later that afternoon. I sobbed together with them, as they laid eyes on the burnt remains of our lovely house for the first time that day.

As the days and weeks passed by, my husband and I became closer as we grieved and prayed together. He listened patiently to my feelings of loss (of our lovely home, our beloved bird), guilt (for switching on the air-con), fear (of the unknown), and gratitude to Allah for keeping our little family safe.

Reflecting on the lessons learnt, I realise that talking to each other was so important in those early days after the incident. I listened to his worries and concerns about the insurance whilst he organised living arrangements going forward. We listened calmly and carefully, without interrupting each other. We poured our hearts out, and went over every detail of the incident, knowing that we could fully trust each other in confidence. *Alhamdulillah* for that, I remember thinking. We also went for counselling as a family. The therapist was very interested in my son's wellbeing, given that he had noticed the fire first. Strange as it may sound, it was good for all of us to talk to an outsider who had no connection to any of us.

I also realised that my husband's manner of grieving differed from mine. He was often quiet and pensive, and occupied himself doing the necessary admin required by the insurance company. On the other hand, I needed to talk about the incident and process the events. When he was not available to listen, I spoke to my friends and family. My parents and sisters supported us during that time, but it was most reassuring knowing that my husband and I had each other. He was my safe place. We talked long into the night, discussing our plans for the children and for us as a family. We prayed together. Remembering Allah in times of distress and thanking Him brought much peace and serenity to us both. As the Quran beautifully reminds us, "Verily in the remembrance of Allah do hearts find peace" (13:28).

Healing takes time. It is not a smooth process. Sometimes he was calm whilst I was agitated; at other times, our roles were reversed. I remained patient and kept reminding myself that this is a passing phase. Many a time, his frustrations and worries differed from mine, and I knew he needed support and a listening ear in those moments. I also recognised when

I needed alone time, away from others and away from distractions. I focused on rejuvenating my soul by making *dhikr*. Being steadfast in uncertain times is a true test from Allah and I worked mindfully at keeping calm and cool. In many ways, knowing that the situation was temporary made it much easier to bear, *Alhamdulillah*.

Lastly, I am glad that we avoided the blame game. It is so easy to fall into this trap, and it is so destructive. As Muslims we know that all things good and bad happen only through the Divine Will of Allah and whatever is meant for us has already been written out and will come to pass. The Quran reminds us, "Allah does not burden a soul beyond that it can bear" (*Surah* 2, Verse 286). Keeping these beautiful words in our hearts and minds reassured us and truly helped us to get through this difficult and trying time.

Pearls of wisdom

Do not allow your attachment to people or the issues of this world distract you from the most important relationship in your life – your relationship with your beloved Creator. Keep your heart focused primarily on Allah. Worldly relationships can come as tests and teachers, and, even with the best of intentions, you can hurt and be hurt. **Rehana Moosajee**

It's okay, this too shall pass. **Afzad-Al**

Talk to each other before taking your problems outside. Most conflict can be solved by better communication. Don't expect your husband to read your mind – ask for what you want. **Aneesa Bodiat-Sujee**

All marriages will experience problems. First try and address these as a couple, before seeking outside help. Often just talking through something together can allay misunderstandings and a solution can be reached. **Raashida Khan**

There will be conflict and hardship in your life! Find common ground and remember that communication is the key to finding a solution to any problem. **Maymoonah Chohan**

Don't stay married just to show the world you are married. If you are compromising your self-respect then it's time to take a long, hard look at your life and that of your child/children. Please don't raise your son or daughter to believe that it's okay for a woman to be disrespected. **Saffiya Ismail Cassim**

Never compare your marriage to anyone else's! Focus on building your relationship, and not on comparing your low points to another couple's highlight reel. **Ayesha Desai**

Hardship and conflict are inevitable. Always maintain profound respect during disagreements and you should be fine. **Razina Theba**

Be the better half always. Don't ever be afraid to apologise, even when you believe you have not erred. **Somayya Hansrod**

Don't get involved in husband-bashing with friends; the negativity seeps into your marriage and affects your relationship with your husband. **Zaheera Jina**

DEALING WITH IN-LAWS

Your mother-in-law is not your enemy. She is not your competitor and never will be.

Nabeela Noorani

A cup of milky white tea
Mumtaz Moosa Saley

The *samoosa* run is not about you and him only. While being allowed time to speak to Mr Eligible alone, Miss Eligible also needs time alone with his mother. Let's face it, we all wish that we had that time to meet dearest mother-in-law. After the *samoosa* run comes the marriage and then it's too late.

Planning the wedding day and getting over the awkward first night is an ordeal and then, just when you think you have it all figured out, you are faced with the nightmare of getting to really know the in-laws. After having heard all the horror stories, you prepare yourself for the terrible worst. Every second woman has already warned you about that nightmare called...the mother-in-law. As a newly married bride, I did not stay with my mother-in-law, but I lived in constant fear of our meetings. I was young, naive and had no clue about cooking or kitchen skills.

Shortly after the wedding day, on a visit to the in-laws, mother-in-law decided to have a cup of tea. As I was still earning my spot, I quickly offered to make the tea. I whipped out the entire kitchen and proceeded to prepare a milky cup of tea. Would it be to her taste? I doubted it. I stood there, looking at the tea, with my heart racing – doof-doof, doof-doof! Would faking a heart attack make my mother-in-law forget about her tea? I was ready to run out the house and never return.

My mother-in-law came in, thanked me for the tea and drank it. Much to my surprise, she smiled and said that she had enjoyed it. I wasn't sure she really meant it, and decided I would practise to improve my tea-making skills.

Although my mother-in-law may not have been honest, she was kind. However, I was still not convinced that she would be good to me, and I waited in anticipation for the monster within her to be unleashed. I had been warned by the 'aunties' that I was now the enemy because I had dared to marry her son. Time went by, and, although we rarely saw each other, my mother-in-law continued to call me every second Sunday to find out if I was well and often sent us meals.

A few months later, when I became pregnant, I took a break from working daily to working only on certain days. I now had time to visit my mother-in-law more often. She took me under her wing, and, with extreme patience she taught me the art of cooking. I know that this was a real challenge for her. Being a mother to four sons, she was the Queen of her kitchen and had not needed to share her space with anybody before my arrival. My mother-in-law gave up her space and time to teach me how to cook and I will always be grateful to her.

Sometimes her patience wore thin. We argued occasionally during my cooking internship, and very occasionally our differences became screaming matches. I remember thinking in horror that I had not only married Yahya but I had also married his mother. Happily, we always made amends.

Nine months passed, and I gave birth to a son. My own mother had passed away when I was only sixteen years old, and my mother-in-law never left my side. When I went home from the hospital I was given a royal welcome. My every need was seen to and taken care of. All I had to do was rest and feed the baby; I didn't have to bath him or change his napkin. My mother-in-law took care of everything.

Two weeks flew by and one day, my mother-in-law had to hurry out to run an errand, and I was left all alone with baby Mikael. I didn't know how to make him stop crying, how to burp him or even how to change him. I became anxious when faced with his soiled napkin. I sat there, promising myself that I would not call my mother-in-law. Instead, I called Yahya who warned me not to move. My mother-in-law arrived soon after, and on that day she taught me how to change Mikael's napkin. Yes, she could have said a million things...but she did not.

My mother-in-law and I have come a long way since then, and today she is not just my mother-in-law but has become my own mother. Like a small girl, I seek her help in everything. She has become my confidant when I need one and my go-to person when I feel lost and alone. My love for her knows no bounds and I would do anything for her. Over the years she could have scolded me so many times, but she has always remained patient with me. Perhaps she still thinks that, if she is not kind to me, I will serve her milky tea!

Yasmin Saley, if I ever get to be a mother-in-law, I pray to take my lead from the kindness you have shown me over the years. You will have to share your secrets with me about how to extend my kindness with overflowing patience.

Your mother-in-law is not your enemy
Nabeela Noorani

I had heard it all before. My own mother had always advised me to accept, love and honour my mother-in-law and to treat her with respect. But unfortunately, I learnt the hard way...

Many would call me lucky. I married a handsome young man not native to our country, which people said would save me from all the 'mother-in-law drama'. My husband took my mother as his own. People termed him the 'son', and me, the 'daughter-in-law' in my own home.

My background is quite neutral. Growing up in Port Elizabeth, one is not often exposed to Indian ways of life. Whether you're Malay or Indian, your upbringing is much the same. However, the man I married was from Kenya and belonged to one of the largest Memon communities in the world.

My first visit to Kenya as a naive, nineteen-year-old bride came as a huge culture shock. I did not get along with my mother-in-law, as she spoke very little English and I can't speak Memon. I cried each time my mother phoned me. I complained endlessly – the diet adding to my unhappiness, as the food was too spicy for my weak tummy.

We returned home four weeks later and life went on. When we left Kenya, my communication with the in-laws ceased to exist. We had a son, visited for another few weeks, and so it went on for a couple of years. Until the time of my second pregnancy.

My mother-in-law developed breast cancer, and my husband brought his parents to South Africa, where my mother-in-law underwent a mastectomy and chemotherapy. It was daunting for all of us. I have high-risk pregnancies, and suddenly, I was responsible for two more adults. Cooking became a necessity, a daily duty, and my nonchalance towards it no longer worked. I blamed my husband – especially for spoiling me before their arrival. The tension that resulted started to ruin our marriage.

Looking back, I know I was being a selfish, immature woman, and I feel embarrassed about how faithless and selfish I was. But at the time, I was drowning in self-pity. I craved sympathy from others for my problems.

Life became so stressful that I packed my bags and found myself with a three-week-old baby boy, crying my heart out in my parents' home. I had got to the point where I was discussing custody of my boys. However, eventually, because of my parents' persistence, I decided to make my marriage work.

A year ago, we made a temporary move to Kenya. The tables turned and I entered my mother-in-law's den. My mother-in-law accepted me with open arms. She never scolded me, never hinted that she was unhappy with me, and never commanded me to work in her house. She treated me better than her own daughters. Her behaviour to me only made me feel more guilty.

I realise now that I could have saved myself so much heartache, had I accepted my mother-in-law fully from the start, the way she accepted me.

Our relationship has grown, and, even though I have now learnt to speak Memon, like peeling off the layers of an onion, there is so much more I would love to discover about my mother-in-law. There will always be a cultural divide, but we are all different, which only adds to the beauty of living with others.

When leaving Kenya, I bought boxes of Arabian perfumed incense to give as gifts. My mother-in-law gasped when she saw them and advised that I must not give them as gifts, as they are said to be aphrodisiacs. We laughed together about it and even though the idea sounded preposterous to me, I respected her advice.

So my advice to young prospective brides is this: Your mother-in-law is not your enemy. She is not your competitor and never will be. Treat your mother-in-law with the respect that you would offer others, and, even if she does not return your love, persist, because your reward lies with your Creator. Hearts are won over with kindness and sweet words.

34 Dealing with in-laws
Zara Valli

As I write this narrative, I reflect back to the time when I was a newlywed, just out of school, and my life changed from living with my parents and siblings to living with my in-laws. I have to admit that I was lucky that my mother-in-law treated me well. My sister-in-law, who was married to my husband's brother, also lived with us, and between them they taught me how to cook. Since I had not cooked much in my mother's house, I learnt to do things the way they showed me, which was the way my husband's taste buds were seasoned.

Although we all got on well and managed just fine together in the kitchen, we had our share of problems, like most families do. At first I found it a challenge to get used to my new family and surroundings. My mother-in-law loved doing things her way, so obviously there were times of conflict. I realise now that I was young, stubborn, petty and naive and I could not see the bigger picture, so little things sometimes became big problems. We sorted out our disagreements and did not hold grudges, and, as the years passed, my mother-in-law and I shared a very close relationship. If I complained about my husband to her, she scolded him and we thereafter laughed about it.

A few years later, while I was pregnant with my second child, my sister-in-law's husband passed away, so she moved back in with us. At first, everything was fine, but as time went on, conflict raised its ugly head. As the saying goes, 'too many women in one kitchen are cause for concern'. At this point, my husband and I decided to move out. My father-in-law was upset with our decision and requested that we stay and help care for the extended family.

I could have argued that we should not have the responsibility of this burden, and insisted on moving. But, in fact, we felt honoured to be given this responsibility. We stayed, with the compromise arrangement that I would get my own kitchen in the upstairs section of the house, which later became my quarters. We still ate some meals together. From this experience I learnt that we must always try to keep the family together and mend family bonds, rather than break them. When I reflect back now, I think that we passed a test that Allah had set out for us.

Yes, I have had issues with my parents-in-law and sisters-in-law, but we have managed to resolved all of them. Sometimes people may be going through their own problems in life, which we may not be aware of, so we should be patient and speak kindly. Harsh words and false accusations can break family ties.

I have been married for over twenty years and my father-in-law and mother-in-law have left this world, but I will always hold them in my prayers. My sister-in-law and her two children, who are now adults, are still living with us. This is Allah's test for me and my husband, to care for them until they can manage on their own; and I hope to pass this test, as I see it as a gift bestowed upon us from above. Remember to look for the silver lining within every problem you face, as Allah will not give you a bigger burden than you can bear.

35

I married his family and they married me...
Zaheera Jina

In Muslim South African Indian folklore the saying goes that 'you don't only marry the boy, you marry his entire family!' For me this saying became my reality and I welcomed it with open arms.

I grew up in a small nuclear family with my parents and two younger brothers. My mother's parents lived in Botswana and when we were young we used to spend the December holidays with them. I have happy memories of *Naani* carrying me on her back, like a bag of potatoes, and offering me to *Naana* for a price. *Naana* stocked his cupboard with chocolates and all the new movie releases for us to watch.

My father's family was scattered in small towns all over Mpumulanga and we visited his parents in Carolina on religious holidays. These visits were always riddled with anxiety because my mother, who was a working woman, scrambled to find time to make the delicacies that she was expected to take with. *Daadi* spoke only Gujerati, and, because I saw so little of her, we shared no bond. *Daadi* was a strict man, feared by everybody. I remember him staying in his room whenever we visited. He would sit there alone and listen to the radio or read the newspaper, and we greeted him from the doorway. Every Eid, *Daadi* would give us a R15 cheque for my two brothers and me to share.

So, when I married into this big extended family of in-laws I received the experience with enthusiasm. I have my own space, but within the house live my mother-in-law, brother-in-law, Aunty Salvia* and Muhammad, Aunty Salvia's son. My sister-in-law, Hasina, was still single and she became the sister I never had. My mother-in-law is a genuinely warm human being who has accepted me as her own daughter. She also accepted Muhammad, and brought him up from birth.

Before my wedding day, my dear *mamajee* wrote me a letter of advice that would prepare me for marriage: "Marriage, you must understand, is a very big step in life; in fact bigger than you ever imagined. You are entering a new world, expecting a great deal of adjustments from you. Unfortunately, the adjustment on your part will have to be greater than that required by your husband. But the important thing to remember is that, the more willing you are to adapt, the happier your marriage will be." *Mamajee* was particularly worried about me staying with a mother-in-law. In his letter he went into detail about the dynamic relationship between all three key players – husband, wife and the mother-in-law. In point form, he wrote:

   a. When your husband compares your cooking with his mother's, do not get upset. It is not that his mother is a better cook, but that is how his taste buds have developed. Don't be shy to learn a few things from her and supplement them with your ideas. That will certainly make you a better cook in the long run.

b. Never complain to him about his mother, e.g. what she said, did or did not do. It is very difficult for a man to take sides between his mother and his wife. So don't force him to, because you are most likely to come second.

c. Never ever be jealous of his love for his mother. He will love you both in different ways, so be content to share him with her and other members of the family. You will lose nothing by it but have a lot to gain.

d. Do not be surprised if his mother is subconsciously jealous of you. If you look at it from her point of view, you will be more understanding. Until you came along, she was the only woman in his life. So, if you note a trace of cattiness, repay it with kindness. No matter how old he is, he will always be a child to her, for as long as she lives.

I was fortunate not to have any of these issues in my marriage. My mother-in-law is very easy when it comes to cooking and eating. We share recipes – I introduced my mother-in-law to *khowse* and she taught me to cook *kheema-kow* the way my husband enjoys it.

In his letter, *Mamajee* also advised:

e. Never make negative remarks to him about your family or his. These things can be thrown back at you at a later stage when there is a serious argument. Be cheery whenever it comes to family matters, irrespective of how you feel inside.

f. You will sooner or later hear, directly or through other sources, negative comments made about you by some of his family members. Overlook them and continue acting as normal, if you wish not to be miserable. In family matters, one has to swallow one's pride. It will hurt less than living with antagonism and hatred.

Mamajee was right about adjustment on my part being greater than that required by my husband. My mother-in-law has four sisters and they became part of the living with in-laws experience and so did their children and grandchildren.

At our engagement, when Aysa *masi* greeted me, she announced that I will need to learn to play the game of poker, because that is what the family did on Saturday nights when they all met for supper. "You cannot take my Sulix away from us, you hear?" she said, wagging her forefinger at me.

I became apprehensive, because I had never played poker before but Suleiman assured me that he would teach me and I was up for the challenge. On Saturday mornings my husband's nephews and nieces come to him for mathematics tuition. And on Saturday nights we all meet at 'big house' where two of my mother-in-law's sisters lived, for supper. Each family takes a turn to make supper for everybody. When it is my turn, I buy pizza. The men take their meals at the dining room table, while the women and children sit in the lounge on the sofas and on the floor and balance their plates on their laps.

After supper, the daughters-in-law wash the dishes and clean up, while their mothers-in-law play board games. At the call of the *esha adhan* the men go to the *masjid* for *salaah*. The women read prayers at home and when the men return everybody gathers around the dining room table for a game of poker. I enjoy these evenings and I quickly became skilled at the game of poker.

Experiences of these meetings extend to savoury making before *Ramadaan*, where all the daughters-in-law and their mothers-in-law meet at 'big house' to fill samosas, pies and moons. They work together, like in a factory, to get the task done. This practice was foreign to me, and, with small children, I sometimes do not go. I listen to the complaints when they are thrown my way and sometimes I argue my worth but mostly I laugh it off. I keep the peace in that way. I cannot make enemies now as I have yet a lifetime to live with my many in-laws. Contrary to *Mamajee*'s wise words, though, I do discuss these confrontations with my husband, because I value his advice and I need his support.

The experience of living with in-laws became a culture shock for me when I experienced my first *Eid-ul-Adha* as a new bride. The complete family of mothers-in-law, daughters-in-law, husbands and children meet at the farm to make the *qurbani*. They pack a picnic basket of drinks and savouries and wait for everybody to do the *qurbani* before leaving. The farm is muddy and pools of blood and mud, mixed, form under the hanging carcasses.

On that first Eid, my brother-in-law cut out a sheep's eye and bisected it for the children to see. I was horrified and nauseous. The next day, fifteen large orange crates full of sheep's meat decorated the tiled floor in my mother-in-law's kitchen. Armed with my knives, I bravely went to help cut, clean and sort out the meat, but soon found out that my mother-in-law preferred to do this ritual with Aunty Salvia at her side. Today, while I still find these practices repulsive, my own children enjoy the whole *qurbani* experience with their cousins.

I am thankful that my children are growing up in a big, happy family. As children, my brothers and I were mostly alone. My mother always prepared a full meal for Eid breakfast, and, after eating, my father would rush off to open the shop. I would make myself comfortable in bed with a mug of tea, a slice of chocolate cake and a novel. In the late afternoon, my *gorikhala* – my mother's cousin – would arrive and we always went with her to visit her father who was also *Naana*'s brother. We called him Baaji. My parents raised us alone, with family support from only my *gorikhala*.

My life is different from my mother's. I have support from all my many in-laws. My mother-in-law helps daily by playing with my children. Little Isa has his early morning cup of tea with *Daadi*. Yusuf collects snails in the garden and helps plant and water the garden with *Daadi*. My children love their *daadi* and she loves them.

The extended family is also always available to help. When my car broke down, it only took one phone call, and my husband's nephews were there to help. When my baby was in hospital, my husband's aunt, who is a neonatal nurse, supported us tirelessly through the days and nights, while my mother-in-law held fort at home, caring for my other two children. So, while I have had to adjust to living with so many new people, I am thankful for the experience. I may have married the entire family of in-laws, but on the flip side, I am proud to say that they have married me, too.

---

* Aunty Salvia is the domestic worker who has been living with the family for 30 years, to date.

Pearls of wisdom

• •

There is never a need to recreate a Zee-Tv soap opera production in your life. Always maintain your dignity; you will be loved and appreciated for that. **Razina Theba**

Be optimistic, they may turn out to be amazing.
Aneesa Bodiat-Sujee

Become a part of your new family as soon as possible. Address your parents-in-law as your husband does (Ma/Oomi/Mom). Learn their culture and traditions and honour them, as you also show them yours by example.
Raashida Khan

Do not let the word 'in-laws' give you a preconception. They are unique, and different to you and your family. So befriend them and avoid confrontation at all costs.
Maymoonah Chohan

Don't make your in-laws an obstacle and burden in your life and don't ever force your spouse to choose between them and you. **Somayya Hansrod**

Be true and honest, even if your in-laws are not. And remember, it's okay to limit contact with toxic people.
Afzad-Al

You set an example for your children to follow. If you treat your in-laws with respect, then your children will learn and follow your lead. Always remember that you are growing older, too, and your turn to be a mother-in-law will happen. Do unto others as you would have them do unto you.
Zaheera Jina

INTIMACY, BABY-MAKING AND CHILDREN

There is a difference between the sharing of bedroom secrets and educating people on bedroom secrets, with taste and class.

Papatia Feuxzar

My 'first night'
Afzad-Al

On the eve of my 30th anniversary, I reflect on how far I've come on this journey called life; and the one thing that stands out is the physical aspect of my marriage. You'd think that after three decades with the same man I'd have reached a comfortable and satisfying level of intimacy with my husband. Alas it isn't so.

I married in my early twenties. Ours was an arranged marriage (so common at the time). My interactions with the opposite sex were mainly with my family and extended family and boys that were with me in school. Our interactions were mostly the 'Hi and Bye' kind.

I grew up reading Sweet Valley High, Mills & Boons, Danielle Steel and Nora Roberts happily-ever-after stories: girl meets guy; they fall in love; they have a misunderstanding and fall out; they resolve their issue, get back together and live happily ever after. So clichéd, right? Yet I was addicted to these books. (Who am I kidding; I still love a feel good book.) So, perhaps it was with these stories in my head that I went into my marriage with high expectations.

My 'First Night', I found myself in the room that was to contain my marital bed in the months to follow. Right next door to my mother-in-law and father-in-law; talk about AWKWARD. So, now I'm not only anxious about 'doing the deed'; I'm worried about how I'm going to face this house of people the next day. People that I've met only once before, the day my father accepted the proposal.

Eventually, his family leave the room, and here I am with this man whom I made *nikah* with, but a stranger nonetheless. My husband locks the door and I'm thinking: is he afraid someone will barge in or that I will run out? (Years later, as I got to know him and his family, I realised that it was a combination of the two.)

There were no 'sweet words' or even getting to know each other. Nor did I know that I had a right to wait and get to know him, get to feel safe and comfortable with him. Little did I know that my naivety and ignorance were going to be my detriment and that his actions were going to set the tone for our marriage.

My husband's understanding of foreplay was a few kisses and rough handling of my body, especially my breasts. My first experience included no fireworks, the earth did not move; in fact I was quite stressed. You see, I didn't bleed that night and I think it strengthened my husband's suspicious nature. Oh! I felt pain and discomfort, but I couldn't voice it, afraid that my cries would be heard in the house. Also, unknown to me at the time, I have a condition that affects the nerves, so pain is increased.

I had slight bleeding after being intimate for three weeks. In all that time, my husband hadn't actually penetrated me fully. Sadly, to this day, he still doesn't know when he's in, and, with combined health issues, I just let it be.

Living with someone whose 'love language' is sex and more sex, irrespective of whether I was pregnant, lactating, on my menses or recovering from flu or a broken ankle, it was always about his gratification. My whole body was fair game: not only my vagina, but between my legs, between my breasts and even anally. Through my ignorance and determination to please him I inadvertently enabled and encouraged this behaviour. My husband used to love porn or anything related to it. So, instead of finding my erogenous zones he was living his life in erroneous ways.

I did not know that marital rape exists, that a wife has a right to say NO! That when something doesn't feel right or comfortable, you are not compelled to comply. Know your rights, educate and empower yourself. If something doesn't feel right, follow your gut instinct. Sexual intimacy is a gift that needs to be enjoyed, revered and respected by both parties. It's not about 'Wham, bam and not even a Thank You, mam'. When done in the correct manner, our Creator is pleased with us.

On my journey, I have learnt important things about intimacy and physical interaction.

I've learnt that a person's hymen can break in their youth, due to physical activity, such as swimming or horse riding.

I've learnt that suspicion and spousal insecurities often lead to arguments and can cause major issues.

I've learnt that grooming is vital and that both spouses should make an effort to be presentable to each other. It's not only a woman's job to look and smell good.

I've learnt that the saying 'the angels curse that woman who has denied her husband's conjugal rights until the next morning'* only applies if you were being spiteful and manipulative.

I've learnt that you have a right to say 'No', and that an understanding and caring spouse will respect your decision.

I've learnt that, if your husband constantly nags and complains about issues of finance, your dress style, your methods of parenting, and the time you spend with either side of the extended family, this can and will impact on your intimacy.

I've learnt that a husband's diatribe creates a distance, a chasm and a feeling of indifference.

I've learnt that people stay in these relationships initially for the children's sake, and that, later, they find a way to just live. I'm taking each day as it comes.

* Reported by al-Bukhaari, 4794.

Too painful to be pleasurable
Anonymous

Long before the 'walk-in, walk-out' function venue that is trending in our communities, wedding week used to be a gathering of the clans, where the *naanis* and the *chotifoois* oversee the preparation of the *gulab jamun*, the *mithai*, the cleaning of the chickens and the preparing of the ingredients before the cook descends to work her magic over *dhegs* laid on open fires. One week – glorious for some, intrusive for others – of renewing family recipes and family bonds, and all round clan-chaos.

For us, the younger generation, wedding week first meant outside playtime with cousins; then it meant work, running to fetch scissors or convey messages; and then, as we grew up, too, it meant attending to the bride. The closer we got to the bride, the closer we got to hearing the whisperings and advice of the inner circle around her.

Our *apakhala* would provide a spectrum of advice. Always add extra chillies to your *akhni*, it's what sets ours apart from everyone else's. Always boil double quantities of *dhal* and freeze it so it's easy when you get unexpected visitors. Make sure you take enough Vaseline – get the biggest tub you can find. When you get to your bedroom, check everywhere for alarm clocks that may have been left to keep you up all night. The laughter would be raucous from the aunties, who in this week seemed to transform from staid to scandalous.

The younger wives in the family would take the bride aside and provide advice. You will need enough Vaseline, it's going to hurt like hell at first but you will learn to enjoy it in time. Make sure he gets his pleasure. And the all-time golden advice: make *sabr*. Whatever the issue: make *sabr*.

All these snippets we heard became the information and misinformation we took to our own marriages.

Three months into mine, Aslam and I had thoroughly enjoyed our honeymoon backpacking through Vietnam. Not for us was the regular beach honeymoon – we took local buses and tasted the local flavours, being the adventurers that we are. But one terrain remained unconquered: breaking my hymen. It was like hitting a brick wall, he said, every time he rolled over in frustration. Twenty-seven-year-old virgins we were, unable to complete the marriage rite that would bond us as husband and wife.

I spoke to my cousin who had heard of something similar, where *jadoo* had been done on the couple. I spoke to our local *aalim*, who referred me to both an *aamil* and to a doctor. The *aamil* – well let's not go there. As the doctor did an internal – or attempted to do an internal – I crossed my legs and flinched. After checking there was no infection, she referred me to a gynaecologist and a sex therapist, Dr Elna McIntosh*.

In therapy, I learnt to do breathing exercises and Elna took me through word associations. First, innocent ones, like pizza and flowers, then to the more loaded ones, like hymen and virginity. When my legs crossed again just at the mention of these, she took me back to my childhood. Two strong memories came back: one of seeing a girl in hospital in traction with her legs splayed open; another of wedding week banter and the mention of that blasted bottle of Vaseline...

Dr MacIntosh's diagnosis was that I had vaginismus** due to an overdeveloped pain phobia. Yes, I came from a traditional culture, she said, and vaginismus was common in societies where sexuality was shrouded in taboo and collective misinformation became a trigger for phobias. But, equally, she informed me, vaginismus is as prevalent in societies where sexuality is open and children may be exposed to it at too young an age.

Back to the gynaecologist, to rule out any other cause. Back to the *aalim*, who counselled us. Back to Elna. The circle repeated. Treatment continued. I received vials that I needed to insert in order to adjust to penetration. Every intimate encounter needed a half-hour preparation alone with the vials, and, in spite of it, no intercourse. I read Aslam's frustrations with a flawed wife into every fight, every tiff, every disagreement, whether rightly or wrongly.

In the meantime, desperately needing an outlet and a way to grow, I resigned from my work in corporate business and started attending Islamic classes at a *madressah* for women. Slowly, in time, I learnt to redefine making *sabr*. Make *sabr*, yes, and work for change. Make *sabr*, yes, and speak up. Make *sabr*, yes, and be courageous. It was not, as I had been taught, make *sabr* and serve up that *sojee* with a smile! And through the *fiqh* and the *fatwahs* of the chapters of *tahaarah* and *nikah*, I slowly learnt to relearn sex education.

Then, one day, encouraged by the *aalim* to take an active role in my recovery, Aslam came to therapy with me. Elna spoke to us about other couples with the same problem. Those where the husband was vested in the treatment made the most rapid recovery. Aslam's expression shifted as he soaked it in. We went out for pizza and then spontaneously took a road trip and booked in at a guest house we found along the road. Spontaneously, he reached for the vials and inserted them. Spontaneously, we moved from outer-course to inter-course.

And although our journey to pain-free intercourse has not been spontaneous – it has involved years of preparation and treatment for my anxiety and to overcome my pain phobia – in time, we too, have come to enjoy pleasurable, pain-free penetration.

To others with the same condition, please be a pilot in your journey to overcome vaginismus. As a *Muslimah*, the idea of seeing a sex therapist may seem taboo, but, guided by a reputable *aalim*, we learnt that it is another form of medical treatment.

To the aunties and older wives whispering advice about the wedding night, please consider what you are teaching and the phobias you may be entrenching.

And finally, to the husbands who may read this, please be a vested partner in your wife's recovery by building her self-esteem.

---

* Although other details have been changed to protect the identity of the writer, Dr Elna McIntosh is a bona fide therapist with a high success rate for treating vaginismus.

** Vaginismus is a condition that causes the pubococcygeus (or PC) muscle to spasm and makes penetration painful or even impossible. It is an involuntary reflex, much the same as the way the eyes blink to protect them from foreign objects or the body flinches when anticipating pain. It occurs beyond the control of the woman. Unfortunately, instead of protecting against pain, it produces pain.

The etiquette to follow for the nuptial night

Papatia Feauxzar

When He made the marriage act between *Hadrat* Fatima and *Hadrat* Ali, our beloved Prophet Muhammed (PBUH) stated: "O Ali! When you take your bride to your house, remove her socks from her feet. Wash her feet. Scatter that water to all corners of the house. By doing this, Allah will remove 70 kinds of poverty from your house, incorporate 70 kinds of *barakah* (prosperity) to your house, and descend 70 *rahmat* (blessings) to you. Together with the bride and her favours, they will reach all corners of the house. Thus, the bride will be secured from insanity and other types of illnesses." (Manaqib-al-Jaleela*)

The bride and groom should not neglect the *hadith*. The wedding night is a very important night for a Muslim couple. It sets the tone for the many nights, days, weeks, months, and years to come. The new couple can prepare for this night by doing research. They can also ask their family members. The groom should talk to a man he trusts to get some advice.

There is etiquette to follow for this nuptial night. The place must be selected in advance. Try not to make it a last minute arrangement;

preparation is key to a successful nuptial night. The nuptial room must be isolated from nosy individuals to give the newly married couple privacy.

The newlyweds should be emotionally, mentally and psychologically prepared for this night by fostering good feelings toward each other. Once the mind is prepared, everything else comes naturally. The newlyweds need to be clean, as cleanliness is the foundation for a successful night. Both parties must wear clean and comfortable clothes.

It may be, after all the preparations for the wedding day, that the first night is non-sexual. The newlyweds may be so exhausted from the wedding ceremonies, that they just fall asleep. Neither party should despair, because this is quite normal and has benefits. They may perform better on another day, when they are fresh. The groom and the bride need to open their ears to each other. They need to be sweet and loving to each other, to dissipate any tension or awkwardness in the room. They should avoid silly quarrels or backbiting. Both parties must try to participate in the act to make it more enjoyable for them.

The first night may also be a time of excitement for the new couple, after several months or even years of waiting for that special day; and having experienced only supervised or chaperoned meetings.

Before the act takes place, the groom should not be vulgar or pounce on the bride right away. He must pace himself with her because she is a delicate flower and it is her right to be treated gently. The groom needs to notice whether she is coy and timid, and, if she is, he needs to take things slowly and make her comfortable. A conversation is a great way to loosen her up.

In addition, the groom should not force his bride into showing her whole self to him. He should dim or turn off the light, if that makes her more comfortable. He should caress her gently to put her in a loving mood or gently corrupt her senses. Being nice, playing nice, touching her with delicacy is the key to her heart. If she is properly aroused and lubricated by his touch, he won't hurt her. She will enjoy it as much as him.

The groom can also research the erogenous zones, as caressing these parts may make the experience more enjoyable for his bride. The bride will loosen up and start enjoying herself if she is properly stimulated by her husband. Penetration will be easy if the wife is wet or lubricated, and an off-the-counter lubricant can be used to facilitate the contact.

The tearing of the hymen by the penis, once inside, will often cause some bleeding and discomfort to the bride. The groom needs to keep caressing his bride to ease her pain and calm her nerves, as she may be tense during this phase. Remember, not all virgins bleed. Some women bleed during their first night and some don't, due to other circumstances, such as horse-back riding, falling, genetics, etc.

The groom should avoid any vulgarity toward his wife. There are too many testimonials from newlywed brides who have not been satisfied on their first and successive nights because they were pounced on or attacked brutally by their husbands. This is sad and should be remediated. However, it is hard to do so because these subjects have become taboo in our society. There is a difference between the sharing of bedroom secrets and educating people on bedroom secrets, with taste and class.

It is quite normal for the nuptial night to be a disaster. For example, it is normal for the groom to experience an orgasm as soon as he comes into contact with his new wife. The new wife should comfort and reassure her husband when this happens. The newlyweds should give it another try and not beat themselves up over it. Perfection comes with practice and patience, the majority of the time.

The groom should do everything in his power to give an orgasm to his bride. He must be patient and see to her needs before his. A woman shouldn't be an object to satisfy her husband's needs. If the bride is not satisfied, she will always be clingy, and it can create infidelity or unhappiness issues down the road. The bride must also communicate her feelings with her groom to help in subsequent sexual encounters.

It must be remembered that every couple may experience performance issues every so often. The couple can research *halaal* positions but must never cross the sodomy line.

If the nuptial night is successful, the couple must rejoice and be happy because this is a bonus for their relationship. They must pray together to Allah for a happy and successful marriage life in the future. *Aameen.*

---

* Manaqib-al-Jaleela is a book on Islamic jurisprudence (*fiqh*) written by twentieth-century Islamic scholar, Mohammad Abdul Ghafoor Hazarvi. This book deals with the observance of rituals, morals and social legislation in Islam, according to the Hanafi School, spreading over nine volumes.

Sublime strawberries
N. Moola

It was certainly not our anniversary, neither was it a birthday or any sort of celebration. It was an ordinary day, ten years into our marriage. Like wilted petals we continued our early evening routines. A dull exploration of the grocery cupboard yielded a rather pasty looking tin of tuna and a dozen stale rolls. Time and exhaustion had run their course during the day as we worked to sustain the rental and nourish the electricity bill. For years, the clichéd, repetitive cycle of working eight to five had stomped the life and breezy energy out of me.

Intimacy belonged to the newlyweds and honeymooners and the young and fabulous, not to me. I was long past intimacy and the phase of being a sassy little kitten. I was older, married to my job, and my husband had become secondary. On that particular day, I adjusted my beige, loose and frayed eight-year-old, extra-large panties that never really stayed in place and walked to snap on the television, so I could have a few minutes of me-time. Me-time was, in fact, a few minutes lodged in front of the plasma, glued to some soapie and munching on some unhealthy item from the snack cupboard.

I had just sunk into the discoloured settee, when the doorbell rang. The ringing of the bell and hollering that went with it beckoned my attention. It was the fruit and vegetable guy. You know, the kind who sells you everything, from yellow-at-the edges *dhania* to mint that bears the scent of decayed citrus. A day later than the market, but a whole lot cheaper. The wandering fruit and vegetable guys have a tender way of selling us their wares amidst amorous bargaining, price slashing and even a bit of corruption. It wouldn't be fair, though, if I didn't mention how their merchandise tends to supplement the dinner table. A fruit here, a fleshy veggie there and the meal morphs from pasty tuna into a delectable curry. On this particular day, though, the hollering fruit and vegetable guy altered my day, my dinner table, my life, my marriage.

After hurrying him away, I piled the goodies onto the wooden table sheathed by a faded pink tablecloth. I stared in disbelief at the mound of fruit I had collected. The fruits were fresh and not at all discoloured. I took in the colours and breathed in the scents. The strawberries were sweet and tangy: plush, red, fleshy heart-shaped delicacies that inspired me. The plump swell of the grapes still attached to their vines dug deep into my imagination. I sank my molars into sweet citrus and shut my eyes as a burst of flavour sizzled on the tip of my tongue. Suddenly, I knew what I had to do.

Luring him into the bedroom proved easy. The burst of colour brought in by the wandering fruit and veg guy was my most unlikely inspiration. On that particular evening, I shed the beige panties; I even shed a tear. I broke the stereotype. I didn't ask him to make love to me; I didn't expect him to make love to me. It was I who made love to him. I made the first move. It was a night unlike any other. I bit onto his upper lip, a burst of citrus. His tongue, like a vine, danced around mine. His fingers, lithe across my breasts, felt like a thousand flitting fleshy pink petals that caressed my thighs, my soul. Strawberry kisses tingled upon my lips, as my entire being sprouted to life.

Why do we always expect to be made love to when we have the power to thrust forth life? That night, I unlocked my potential to truly love someone. The intimacy was different; the end of a decade of dormancy. Like the volcano, Vesuvius, every cell within me exploded. I touched and he gasped. I bit onto the curve of his neck and he bit back. Our fingers entwined and our eyes met and locked. It was not just a moment of pure bliss; not just a physical climax but a deeper connection: the connection that we lose when we are consumed by babies, diapers, in-laws, work, traffic and routines.

Those moments when you are entwined within each other's grasp are the moments you should bathe in, savour in and absolutely revel in. As he gently slid into me, around me, my world opened into a brightly coloured tunnel of flashing purple and yellow light, fluttering butterflies and swaying orange moons, my chipped nails ripped into his back and sank deep into his perfumed skin. It was beautiful.

It dawned upon me that love has no boundaries in a marriage. Love transcends looks and figures, money and beige panties. Love is deeper than sex; it is pure, unfiltered deep gratification and gratitude that extends to beyond the soul, out into the universe.

Funny that an unsuspecting vendor had such a deep lesson to teach me. Our most precious lessons come from the most unlikely sources. We are all guilty of owning that one-size-too-big top, the old grimy sneakers, the mud-caked clogs, the frayed, sagging bra, the *burqah* with the holes, and, of course, the few-sizes-too-big beige panties. When we need to progress, a little tightening of the elastic is needed. If you, too, can learn a lesson from tender strawberries and beige panties, then you, my friend, have learnt a valuable lesson in life.

Life, lies and liberation
Quraisha Dawood

In life, you will tell yourself a few lies:
Matric is the hardest I will ever work.
My life will be set after I get married.
I don't need a mother's advice.

The trouble with life is, it lets you go on innocently believing yourself until you're pulling your hair out over university psychology; making adult decisions about furniture and finances; and calling your mom on your honeymoon because your hubby has been in the loo for longer than you have been married and there are no pharmacies nearby to remedy his food poisoning (#truestory #wasnotmycooking).

As humorous as these lies may sound now, I can guarantee that finding out the truth is not fun. And to those still living under a spell, God protect you from the coming revelation.

***

I must say that in the lottery of husbands, I won big. Shy Shiraz, with his dimply smile and engineer-rationality, somehow understands me, while I am the creative crazy dreamer. He has literally travelled the world with me through my Masters and PhD, yet he always brings me back to earth.

We are both very independent people. My advice to young people is, be a complete person and marry someone who adds to your life. Don't marry someone because you are desperate for completion. Yet, even though I married the man of my dreams, in the last few years I have learnt that life is not at all set after marriage. No matter how independent one is and no matter how strong one's marriage is, one can never predict what tests lie ahead.

I cannot describe the elation I felt the day I found out I was pregnant. We had been trying for a while and the pressure of nagging aunties and my loud biological clock were getting to me. Those two blue lines carried me to an untouchable cloud, and I floated happily around. I was unaware that the twinges I felt were actually an inkling of the pain that was coming. Growing pains, I thought.

But in the weeks ahead, we were told we were 'likely to miscarry'. I couldn't bring myself to even think of the word. I couldn't imagine how someone could carry on with life, after that word became part of their lives. I prayed. I bargained. I raged. There were invasive medications and lingering days of horizontal uncertainty. Finally, we heard silence, where there was supposed to be a heartbeat and I saw blood, when there was supposed to be nothing.

And the pain. Just like my elation, I will never be able to describe it. But it was just the beginning. A wife is never prepared to see her husband's heart break. She is never prepared for the insensitive questions that come afterwards, or invitations to baby showers, or what to call herself on Mother's Day.

Slowly, I opened up to my colleagues. It was cathartic to just talk. I was humbled to find out that three of these high-powered academics had gone through the same thing. They did not let a miscarriage define them, and they are all moms to amazing children now. I found more women like us, among my family and friends and on Facebook. I felt less alone in a world where the topic still seems taboo.

After four months of painful fertility treatment, Shiraz and I resolved that maybe being parents wasn't in our *taqdeer*. Somehow, between working towards my doctorate and filling out visa applications for a conference in Japan, the two blue lines showed up again. The medication I had to take in order to keep my pregnancy made me paranoid, but as my little boy grew stronger and literally kicked me out of my sadness, I began to smile again. My joy was short-lived, as complications and bed-rest took over. But I finally met my gorgeous baby boy, who was born at 34 weeks. Muhammad Armaan.

He was tiny. Too tiny to touch, I worried. My fear and resentment of this new role eclipsed every joyful experience. I kicked and screamed internally under the weight of the responsibility, waiting for that motherly instinct that eluded me. I couldn't write, sleep or talk. My life seemed out of my control, divided into feeding times and diapers.

Muhammad Armaan was a pleasant, quiet baby. People kept telling me how lucky I was. But something was seriously wrong. The hormonal changes had plunged me into postpartum depression and I felt paralysed in darkness, far away from myself, contemplating an escape.

I was hospitalised a few times, my mom and Shiraz taking over my duties. I can't imagine what Shiraz must have felt, but he held on. He was strong, inhumanely so. And for a mother to see her daughter reject motherhood must have shaken my mother's world.

My friends who visited me in that state and sat with me to talk about nothing in particular are my sisters now. And, despite all my independent ideas about the type of mother I would be, I realised how much I needed my own mom. I couldn't believe how strong she was, how caring, how innately mothering she was with my son. As he grows, I wonder where she found the strength to be a single parent of a stubborn girl like me, in a society which still does not give single mothers the reverence they deserve.

I found strength in other mothers, too. My supervisor, Debby Bonnin, showed me empathy and patience that extended beyond the academic deadlines. My work actually became therapy for me – the one thing I could control. She led me to Jenni Johnson of the Baby Clinic, another amazing mom, who helped me get Muhammad Armaan into a routine. Her talks with me were honest and straightforward and I am forever grateful for those visits in which I broke down or triumphed or simply made it through another month. The mothering instincts of my son's nanny are a gift that brightens my home every day. Mothers are truly spectacular. And, as a father, Shiraz is everything I wished for my son, and more.

I am still getting to know myself as a mom. Some days I revel in taking my son to the beach and singing his favourite songs. Other days (and they are getting fewer) I find it hard to make a cup of coffee. I am not the best mother, but I am the best I can be right now. Above all, I am there.

I am grateful for all I have been through and those who have been through it with me. People ask about when we will have more children and say, "Shame, he needs a friend". But the real shame lies in their blindness to all my blessings. I have learnt that it's okay to wait until you're ready. And it's also okay if you are never ready.

The magic lies in your personal journey towards the truth. Somehow, along the way, you will find something emerging from the daunting shadow of society, which is raw and beautiful: yourself. You will bask in your own light until you cannot help be anyone but your authentic self.

41

Difficulties of conceiving

Anonymous

Okay, so nobody told me that making a baby would be so difficult. They did not tell me about ovulation dates or sex positions, or that off-the-counter lubricants kill sperm. I learnt the hard way.

I struggled to fall pregnant the second time round. It refused to happen and I lived in a time capsule of calculations. Every month's show of blood left me sad and incomplete. It's a terrible feeling when you realise that you cannot give your husband that one thing that he desires – a baby. Muslim marriage revolves around making babies, or so it seems when you are desperately trying.

The gynaecologist recommended that we use the albumen of a hen's egg as a lubricant, because it won't kill off the sperm. So, we mastered the art of separating albumen from the yolk, with or without an egg separator. She also prescribed a drug that increases ovulation. When my friend, Fatima, heard, she was angry and bluntly asked if the gynaecologist had done blood investigations before issuing the prescription. She was even more direct when she looked at me in the eye and said, "Wake up ZJ! You are not getting any younger! Only a fertility specialist will be able to help!"

With her encouragement, I made the dreaded appointment. Arriving at the fertility clinic at 6 am, I discovered other infertile beings had arrived in the dark, and were sitting in heated cars, waiting for the doors to open. Once inside, we huddled together, crammed between laptops on the leather seats. Nobody greeted, nobody spoke, and yet we were all there for the same reason. We waited for the specialist to usher two couples at a time into the main office and adjoining rooms. Join the sheep, will you, at the time of slaughtering.

The fertility specialist did a post-coital test and we watched lifeless, dead sperm float under a microscope. The environment within me seemed somewhat toxic and it was killing off the sperm.

A few weeks later I went in for a laparoscopy and was told afterwards that they had lazered out third-stage endometriosis from both of my ovaries. The fertility specialist advised that we could try to conceive 'naturally' for six months only, before the endometriosis would grow again.

My mother-in-law suggested we visit the *Moulana*, who prays on eggs*, which you eat to fall pregnant. Suleiman called him and after writing down our details, he requested farm-bred eggs. The following day, we drove around Lenasia in search of two farm-bred eggs, but to no avail; we returned home empty handed. So we bought Pick n Pay's free range eggs and took them to the *Moulana*. He wrote and prayed on them, and we ate the prayed-on eggs...but they did not help. We did not conceive. (My mother-in-law still laments that, had the eggs been farm bred, the results would have been different.)

During this struggle, I took refuge in the pages of the English Quran and was comforted to read of *Hadrat* Ebrahim and *Hadrat* Zakariyya's quest for progeny. I spent more time with my aged *naani* and we prayed together. I gave out *sadaqah* in eggs, bread, milk and meat. I fasted.

Despite my own mother's better judgement, we then attempted an expensive cycle of in vitro fertilisation (IVF), which involved weeks of ovulation induction, egg retrieval, fertilisation and embryo transfer and implantation. We did the implantation on Eid day. While families were enjoying scrumptious foods, I underwent a procedure where three embryos were transferred via a small plastic tube placed through the cervix into my uterine cavity. And then we waited and prayed for a full two weeks. The longest wait, ever. The IVF process did not work and I later discovered that it seldom works on the first attempt. I was paranoid that the endometriosis would re-grow and became obsessed with eating good food and exercising. Sweet potatoes became my staple diet.

It was then that I discovered Maca, a fertility inducing root that grows in Peru. I googled its benefits and self-medicated, without telling anybody. Maca became my powdered gold, because, after a few months of taking a teaspoonful with my morning breakfast, much to my amazement, I conceived. I gave birth to a healthy baby boy nine months later.

My struggle is not my own to keep. Infertility is a struggle for so many women, and because it is still considered taboo, many women suffer in silence. Women who face infertility need to visit fertility specialists – gynaecologists are not fully qualified to help. Women also need to speak to other women whom they can trust. During this trying time, every woman needs a shoulder to sob on. I am thankful to Fatima for her advice. The world definitely needs more women like her.

* Muslim people may seek the assistance of a *Moulana* when encountering hardships.

42 Baby-making
Anonymous

I never wanted a fancy career or lots of money in my bank account. Neither did I want a fast car or a palace of a house. All I wanted was a good husband and lots of children.

So when I had a *'samoosa* run' and Mr Eligible said, "I want lots of kids", I almost agreed to marriage immediately. I was studying to become a teacher, but as soon as I got married I de-registered. I was ready to be a wife, a home executive and a loving mother.

A year later, when there was no late period, no positive pregnancy test, no nausea, no bump forming on my flat stomach, and no kicks from the inside (I definitely got them from my sleeping husband on the outside), I knew that there was something wrong.

I already had all the 'aunties' asking me when was I bringing babies, offering me advice that I didn't want. It irritated me and I got angry every time they asked me, because I felt that it wasn't their business. My husband, on the other hand, the witty person that he is, always told them, "You make *duah*, because we are making the effort". The poor aunty would blush profusely.

But when we were alone, and I would complain about the nosy aunty, he would always advise me. "They only mean well. Take their advice; you might learn something from them. Tell them to make *duah*, because you never know whose *duah* will get accepted".

At that time, everyone around me fell pregnant. Even some women who had 'closed shop' fell pregnant, but not me. I felt left out of every conversation, no pregnancy symptoms to share, or baby things to talk about. I hated it when a tired mother would tell me to enjoy my sleep, or an expecting mother of two children would complain that she didn't want another baby. I hated that they didn't care to ask if I was trying. I hated that I didn't have an opportunity to tell them to make *duah* that I get a baby. I hated that they were not as inquisitive or as caring as the older women.

My journey to baby-making started off with a GP/obstetrician who did not give any information or advice on falling pregnant. All she said was, "Don't worry, it will happen".

It didn't happen!

With no tips and tricks from her, I resorted to Dr Google. I tried everything I read or heard from the aunties. I ate healthily, took multi-vitamins, did the 'deed' every second night, lay with my legs in the air for an hour, drank 'sacred water'. I even tried steaming my 'lady parts'. Yes! I literally boiled a magic potion of herbs and veggies, put it in a bucket and sat over it, convincing myself that my womb would open up to the herbal *tarkari* that I had concocted.

We 'had sex' only for baby-making and not for pleasure. We did it only when I thought that I was ovulating and at every other time I faked a headache.

It still did not happen!

Eventually, we went to a fertility specialist, where we were requested to undergo many different tests. My husband had to go for a sperm test, which is ego taunting for a man. He remained patient and encouraging. When all the tests came back clear, the doctor put me on a fertility drug called clomid.

It happened!

Yes, I fell pregnant. Finally, I would have a human growing inside me. Finally, I would be a mother. I was told not to tell anyone because of *nazar*, but I told everyone. I was so excited that I could have climbed up the highest mountain and screamed my news to the world. But when I went for my first scan at only eight weeks, there was no heartbeat, there was no baby; there was only an empty sac.

My heart shattered into a million jagged pieces; but I realised that I could be more positive now. I believed that because I had fallen pregnant once, I would again...and six months later, I finally did. But again there was no heartbeat; there was only an empty sac. Again it all ended in heartbreak.

Before we embarked on the third course of clomid, my husband and I decided to take a break from baby-making. We chose not to worry about medication or the study of my vaginal discharge in order to track ovulation. We didn't worry about in which position we had intercourse, or when we did it. Baby-making had killed our passion and we needed to re-ignite it. We enjoyed this break and we rekindled our passion using games and toys. We did everything in accordance with *Sharíah* law.

That month I waited anxiously for my period to come, so that we could start the next round of clomid. Even though we had not been actively trying, I still hounded my period like a woman hounding her cheating husband – agitated and stressed. When my period was only one hour late, my mind had already gone wild with expectations. After two days of anxiety, I finally took the test.

I was pregnant again. I was more worried this time round, so I didn't share my news with anyone. I didn't want to raise my hopes and then have them shattered again. I went for the scan expecting the usual bad news. This time the sac was full and we heard the heartbeat. We cried. In me, a baby was finally growing.

This time was different from the other times. Perhaps it was that our lovemaking had been spontaneous and relaxed. Perhaps the herbal *tarkari* had opened my womb. Whatever the technique, our *duahs* had finally been accepted.

At 38 weeks, on my birthday, I received my gift. My little girl was born and I named her Shaakirah; a reminder of how long it took to get her, to always be grateful for her.

It's been four years since our princess's birth and I am actively trying again for another baby. I thought I would be satisfied with only one child, but Shaakirah needs a sibling. And so I have resorted again to preparing a herbal *tarkari* to steam my womb.

Baby-making is a tough sport but keep faith that Allah will bless you with a child when the time is right. Make *duah*, and seek advice from the elders in your community.

They too have their stories.

When the body betrays
Dilshad Parker

It's week five. Funny feelings in my gut every so often. Every couple of days a cough surprises me and a stabbing pain in my abdomen brings on tears. Fear ties a knot in my stomach. We've come this far, please lord keep this baby safe.

I've only just thought of documenting this. After so much consistent disappointment, writing down anything seemed like a sure way of jinxing things. Besides, who would want to wallow in month after month of waiting and tears after the onset of every period?

The IVF was successful on our first try, a surprise to both of us. We received the first positive test result with tears and disbelief. Too scared to enjoy the moment, and all the while waiting for the other shoe to drop. For the next four days we waited with baited breath, our faces drawn with worry, like two people undergoing some kind of trauma, rather than having received the best news of our lives. At the second positive result we finally expelled the collective breath we'd been holding. Smiling true smiles and crying tears of joy.

Where did it all start? I began with the arrogance of a not-so-young, professional woman who thought misfortune couldn't happen to her. Sure, I'd read the statistics about how it becomes harder to fall pregnant when you're over thirty but I thought all was normal until at least thirty-five, considering I'd always been healthy and had no medical issues to speak of. And then along came a silent, undetectable parasite called endometriosis – the Berlin Wall to getting pregnant.

I was 33 and had been married for three years when we decided to go for broke and ditch the pill and the condoms. We were finally ready for the whole nine yards. The sweet and bad baby smells, the gurgling noises, the weight of responsibility, the nappies, the sleepless nights, all of it.

After a puzzling (read 'in denial') twelve months of trying without success, we decided to see a gynaecologist, who discovered I had endometriosis. This condition, which I knew very little about, seemed to have been lurking inside me for a while. The only way to diagnose it is when it manifests in severe abdominal pain during your period. In the last two years my period had become progressively more painful. I didn't think much of it and would not have known if I had not been trying to get pregnant.

A minor surgical procedure called a laparoscopy was needed in order to remove the offending tissue, which was pulling my ovaries and tubes in all directions, making it impossible for me to fall pregnant. The endometriosis was not supposed to come back for at least two years. Two years passed and still no luck. No amount of counting the right days, sex at the break of dawn, late afternoon, crazy positions or piles of cushions under my backside seemed to make any difference. We decided to see a fertility specialist and take things to the next level.

As a Muslim woman, the idea of not having children was just not to be entertained. Actually that is not true. As a woman, there is an unspoken yardstick by which we are measured and by which we measure ourselves. You don't have to be Muslim to feel the pressure of living up to expectations: to look a certain way, be a certain size, have a boyfriend by age 18, be married by 23 and have three kids by the time you're 30.

I was in no hurry. I had life to live and experiences to have, and, thankfully my parents were not the type to pressurise me into marriage with a 'suitable boy'. I also wasn't the motherly type and never really entertained longing dreams about my family of five and a white picket fence. Even being married at 30 years old did not spur on any sense of urgency about my biological clock, which was slowly imploding. I was enjoying being married, finding who I was outside of my family home, and learning – to my surprise – that sharing myself with another person and spending all my time with him did not diminish me or rob me of my individuality.

To start with, our decision to have a child had been almost purely practical. Life was good. We were both settled in good jobs, had just bought a house. It was the logical next step. But once the decision was made, it was like a switch flipped inside me. Perhaps I dropped something protective that I had unknowingly held in place, but suddenly other people's babies were the cutest thing on the planet. Women with pregnant bellies were everywhere and parents pushing prams with cooing infants would make butterflies flutter in my stomach. I was not prepared for failure.

When I hadn't fallen pregnant after the first year of trying, I still managed to take it in my stride. After no luck the second year, I started questioning my value as a woman. This body with its hidden defect was betraying me. Around me, friends my age seemed to be getting knocked up like there was something in the water. So the problem was just me, right?

I questioned my spirituality, asking Allah, what had I done? Where was I falling short? Was I not good enough? But why? Why was I struggling, when women who did not want babies or could not afford them were giving them away? When I, who had everything to offer seemed unable to have one of my own.

And this continued for five years. Years of seeing fertility specialists, enduring injections and artificial inseminations and experiencing the hormone rollercoaster. The cycle of hope, each time followed with disappointment and beating myself up. Until the one that finally took.

I am still shell shocked. The news of success came with a tsunami of relief rather than joy, which expressed itself in a wave of violent tears in a public space. I am pregnant. I am worthy.

My heart's story
Somayya Hansrod

Two lines appeared. Dull at first. Then, bright, bold, blue! A warm fuzziness enveloped me. Nothing else mattered at that instant. The instant I realised that within me the seed of my Fatima Zahraa had been embedded. Time froze for a moment. A precious moment, as I stood in a smiling silence. Basking in the absolute glory of motherhood.

This was my fourth pregnancy. Naailah, my first, my princess, with a heart as huge as the universe. Uwais, my second born, my feisty fox, full of love and affection. Abdur Rehman, my soldier, a born fighter from his early entry into the world. And soon, nine months soon, my Fatima Zahraa would complete my family. The queen of paradise had entered the most sacred part of my being, my heart. I lovingly glanced at the two lines once more before replacing the stick into its foil packaging and placing it on the uppermost bathroom shelf. This would not be thrown into the dustbin; this would be kept safely, guarded and treasured.

"It is still early," the doctor said at a routine visit. "Too early to detect a heartbeat," she continued, as she glided the ultra sound probe over my belly.

"It is not too early for me," I softly murmured. My heart had already fully and completely welcomed its most recent occupant.

A few weeks' later, as per doctor's instructions, another ultra sound. And there it was, loud and clear: Fatima Zahra's beautiful, rhythmic, pumping heart. A precious melody to my ears. So, so comforting. Engulfed by an overwhelming bond with this most recent inhabitant of my womb, I left the doctor's rooms, pleased and satisfied. Walking to the car, I placed my hand onto my heart, it had grown, my love had extended to include one more.

This pregnancy would be different, this child would be different, I envisaged. Months prior, I had been guided by the Almighty, led to see my errors, inspired to realise my wrongs and, most importantly, steered towards begging for pardon. I was enjoying a most splendid phase of my existence. What an opportune time to bring another being into this world.

My main and only concern was pleasing my Creator. My only desire each day was to attend gatherings of His remembrance and to look for ways that would draw me closer and closer to Him. My baby, my Fatima Zahra would enjoy all of these blessings. How fortunate was she to be hearing Quranic verses on a regular basis while in my womb. "How beautiful will her character be," I often thought, "if she is constantly surrounded by women whose aim is to emulate exemplary women of Islamic history." As my heart filled each day with the glory and power of Allah, I prayed that my baby would have a heart filled entirely and solely with the love for Allah.

Very, very soon, common pregnancy niggles set in. Food cravings topped the list, with great ferocity. At odd hours I would crave for the most unusual kinds of foods. And, to my husband's detriment, these insane and outright ridiculous demands were not for easily available store bought items, like china fruit and NikNaks. But rather they were for my out-of-town aunt's freshly made, light as air, croissants. My desire for these heavenly croissants was so strong that I smelt yeast wherever I went.

These cravings metamorphosed from insanely sweet to heartburn spicy in an instant. I would wake up in the middle of the night desperately wanting to eat strong, green *masala*-rich *khuri* with mince, overflowing with rich gravy and succulent fresh peas. I insisted on having hot *masala* slap chips for breakfast – strong, vinegar-infused café chips, with a generous splashing of red hot chillies. Whereas my heart was infused with an overwhelming love and excitement for my queen's impending arrival, my hips filled generously with all things sweet and spicy.

While still in my first trimester, powerful fatigue set in. I slept at every opportunity that I got. My husband fondly referred to me as his sleeping beauty. I, on the other hand, was convinced that I would transform into Miss World by the end of my pregnancy, if there was any truth in the saying that good sleep was the answer to achieving youthful beauty. I jokingly justified my increasingly long slumbers as highly essential since I wouldn't be getting much sleep with the breastfeeding nights that lay ahead. Two years of breastfeeding meant two years of interrupted sleep, which meant sleeping every two hours now was actually far less than what would be rightfully due to me.

Nearing my 10-week routine check-up, I noticed some discharge each time I visited the toilet. "Just some old blood," a friend said. "Nothing to worry about." So I brushed off my uneasy feeling. When the discharge increased in volume and changed to a very dark colour, panic set in. Immediately I rushed to the doctor's rooms.

"It's a mess!" the doctor said as she pressed the sonar probe on my belly. My body stiffened, my lips trembled. "Please, please look again," I pleaded with a feeble stutter. "There's nothing," the doctor said. "Why didn't you come earlier?" she questioned.

I lay for a few moments, cold, barren, bare. I shivered and trembled, my body's reaction to the tragedy. My legs jerked. My hands shook, out of my control. My mind raced, went blank, froze. "You have miscarried," the doctor said. Miscarried. Miscarried. The words played over and over in my mind.

The drive home was a whirlwind of emotions. Thoughts flooded my mind. The sacred land that had harboured my queen, my Fatima Zahraa, had been gruesomely pierced, stabbed and stabbed again. My heart had been invaded by a force so great, so powerful, it was beyond my control. A pain that I had never felt before surfaced. A hurt that no painkiller could take away followed my every move. I wondered, was this a nightmare? Would I awaken soon to a different reality? I pondered, was the doctor mistaken? Had she erred? Possibly? I would feel a slight flutter again after a few days and all this would be a misdiagnosis. It was possible, even doctors made mistakes. I wouldn't fight, I wouldn't sue. I would have my baby back. A mistake, I would accept it. It would all be okay. This would be over soon. I would have my baby back. I was not in denial. I was not unaccepting.

I was hurting so badly, the tears filled my eyes and flowed down my cheeks with increasing vigour as they turned into torrents. Each outburst increased the pain, penetrating deeper each time. At that moment, I decided no longer would anyone or anything enter my heart. I would guard it forever. Guard it from planning, from foreseeing, from anticipating. No longer would anything claim my love, my affection, my emotions. Overtaken with fatigue, physically and emotionally, sleep brought the tears to a temporary halt, brought my thoughts to a momentary silence.

And when I awoke, they arrived in droves. Family, friends, neighbours, well-wishers, soothsayers, story seekers, rumour mongers, gossip tellers, they arrived, carrying with them judgemental statements, insensitive remarks and stories of lost hope.

"It will be okay," they said. Nothing felt okay for me.

"At least, you have other children," they said. It didn't make the pain go away. It didn't make the tears stop.

"You will fall pregnant again," they said. It didn't make the hurt any less. The tears still flowed.

"Make *sabr*," they said over and over again. But the sadness didn't leave me.

"Get up and move on. You will fall pregnant again soon." My body refused to leave my bed. My heart refused to forget.

Dreadful hours turned into sorrowful days, which turned into forsaken weeks. And one night, as I stirred in my sleep, a force prompted me to leave my bed. Prompted me to rise, to abandon the covers. Prompted me to stand, to perform *wudhu*. Prompted me to prostrate to my Lord and cry and cry and cry till my eyes hurt. A force prompted me to beg. To beg for the pain to be removed, begged for my heart to be restored, begged over and over again for forgiveness. An awakening of enormous magnitude. An awakening of tremendous blessings for my battered heart and my bruised soul.

I vowed that night, that if I ever encounter a hurt or grief-stricken soul, I will say, "Cry, cry, let the tears flow. Your tears do not mean you are not accepting your *taqdeer*."

I will say, "Don't wipe away your tears when you hear someone approaching! Express your emotions, you are not being selfish."

I will say, "Take some time out, a day or two, or more. Removing yourself does not mean you are giving up."

I will say, "Allah has not forsaken you, and neither is he punishing you. He loves you more than you could ever imagine or understand."

I will say, "Don't guard your heart. Just remember, always remember that nothing belongs to us."

I will say...No, I won't say a word, not a single word.

I will hug her; I will hug her with every fibre of my being. I will let her tears flow all over me, I will let them wet my cheeks, soak my hair and stain my clothing. Then with both my hands, my bare hands I will gently, lovingly, carefully wipe away every single tear. And as each tear disappears I will replace it with a comforting word, a reassuring whisper, a gentle kindness, a soft touch. And as I feel her heart beginning to beat a calm, tranquil beat, I will continue to hold on. And as the painful tears turn to soft sobs, I will hold on. And as her body begins to soften and her bones start to ease, I will hold her face within my hands, look deep into her eyes and tell her with utmost sincerity and conviction:

"All with the blessings and mercy of the Almighty, this shall soon pass and you will experience overwhelming tranquillity and sublime peace. Soon you will triumph with a new-found love and adoration, a love that will enter your heart and never, ever depart. Soon, very soon, you will tell your tale just the way I did."

Romance on pause
Ayesha Desai

I have often heard that once you become a mother, you stop being everything else. You hear phrases like 'Motherhood is about sacrifice', about giving things up and losing what you had before. You're told you have to say goodbye to sleep, because babies don't sleep. And goodbye to white shirts, because babies will ruin them. And goodbye to nights out with friends and date nights with your husband. And goodbye to eating a meal in peace...and to so many parts of what makes you as a person, and part of a couple. We start to internalise this and think that the more we lose of ourselves, the more we give up, the lower down on the list of priorities we place ourselves, the better we become at being mothers.

You will undoubtedly miss what you were before you took on that title of mother, mum, mama. But you'll also discover new aspects of yourself. Some days, you will be amazed at your saintly levels of patience and ability to prepare a meal entirely one handed. Other days, you will be horrified at your lack of patience and lack of care about your appearance. One day, when you look in the mirror and see streaks of grey, you'll ask yourself how you changed so much. You'll wonder where the young, energetic version of that face disappeared to. You will wonder what happened to the excitement you used to feel when you saw your husband after a long day. You will miss having uninterrupted, meaningful conversations with the love of your life, instead of conversations about specials on nappies. You'll miss eating together, instead of one eating while the other holds the baby.

And then, when out shopping and you find yourself admiring a pair of beautiful and wholly unsuitable tropical patterned wedge heels, you'll see the old you peeking through the mesh of motherhood and you'll glance back at her and at those shoes wistfully, saying, "I'll buy shoes like that again, one day." And you'll see glimpses of the old you again when your kids go to bed early, and, because you can't sleep yourself right now, you spend an hour texting with old school friends from your pre-mum days. You'll see glimpses of your old love life when he hugs you after you've been puked on for the third time that day, or when he makes you a cup of coffee before he leaves in the morning.

Sometimes, that old you is buried so far beneath the layers of sick kids, exhaustion, constant requests for food, and school schedules that you become convinced she is indeed, lost. Likewise, your love life gets buried under school fees, assembling bicycles, and medicine prescriptions, and you forget the butterflies that got you there!

But, like those missing socks that we think are lost forever but we find behind the washing machine or under the car seat two years later, you were never really gone and your love never disappeared. They have just been put on pause whilst you deal with the immediate urgencies, and are waiting to be rediscovered. Sometimes, they turn up in the most unexpected of places. Sometimes it takes patience and sometimes deliberate work.

Even now that my children are older and conversations with my husband are starting to be about us again, whenever I have to leave my children, even for a few hours, my excitement at the prospect of 'me time' is still tinged with hesitation. Will they be okay? Are they too young? Are we going to be away for too long? Are we being mean parents for not taking them with us? Do we really need this time apart from the children?

I was asked a question a while ago that made me stop and do some serious introspection: Which comes first, your children or your marriage? I was flabbergasted and annoyed because I didn't have an instant answer. I wanted so much to say, "Of course, my children!" But in order for them to come first, I had to be a good parent, and I can't parent alone. I need my husband to parent with me. My need to make my children come first can only be realised if my marriage is a strong one. So, then, does my marriage come first?

This confusing conundrum brought about much clarity in the end. I know now, that in order to keep doing all of the selfless things that parenthood entails, we have to take care of ourselves. It's not a want, it's a need! So much of our role is to anticipate and address everyone else's needs, we forget the foundational building block of a family is the parents' relationship, which, in turn, rests on their needs as individual people and to feel part of a team, a couple.

I've realised that I don't necessarily have to have huge amounts of time by myself for this to happen. Sometimes it's as simple as giving yourself the permission to finish your coffee, even when your child is waiting for you to tie his shoelace. Sometimes it's as simple as sending your man a message in the middle of the day and getting an instant reply. It's as simple as cooking sugar beans and *roti* for supper just because you're craving it, knowing the children will inevitably have toasted cheese sandwiches instead – but, hey, once in a while there's nothing wrong with treating yourself.

When it comes to your marriage, know that relationships change. People change. But if that change happens together, whilst still keeping your eye on the goal, it is easier to adjust to. The days of flowers and chocolates and extravagant romantic gestures might be gone, but always make time to reinforce the marriage, too. Your needs as a couple are just as important as your children's.

Once you lazed about on weekends and spontaneously did whatever you wanted, living the easy life. It might not be as easy now, but if you work at it, it can still be good! Moments of connection and belonging are different, but they need to be acknowledged. Like your shared pride and celebration when your boy scores the winning goal, or being woken up by little, excited voices saying, "We're going on holiday today!" It's that unexpected hour of quality time when the kids fall asleep in the car on the drive home and you smile at each other; or when you sit in the dark, hoping the kids are asleep but you're not sure, so you conspire to share a packet of chips as silently as possible and your fingers brush against each other; or when you're both watching their rare peaceful interactions in silence, while they're unaware of you looking on, and you're thinking "Look at our family!" but when he turns to you, he says "I love you!"

Look for these moments, savour them. It's moments like these that build love. It's this love that builds a family.

Raising kids in the 21st century
Fatima Kazee

I remember when I was a little girl, in the 80s. We used to play for hours in the streets with our friends, until my mother or grandmother had to call me in because it was getting dark. Climbing the neighbour's tree and onto his roof to see what we thought was the rest of the entire country. Street soccer, where the boys always cheated the girls into believing that they were better. 'Elastics' and hop-scotch. I even recall one time when three of us decided to climb into the yard of the only aunty on the street that had a pool. She wasn't there, so we made ourselves at home, towels laid out, splashing around in her pool. She came home, of course, to find us there and it was complete pandemonium! I don't think I'd ever scaled a wall that fast in my life...or ever needed to since!

So, coming back to 2017, I can tell you one thing, for sure – kids of today are a whole different kettle of fish. Not only do they need to be stimulated every hour of every day but they also nag – a lot! When we were little, we were just given one disapproving look and we would be timid little puppies, sitting quietly, without any further eye contact. Today, its arguments and explanations, and the simple "because I said so" doesn't work anymore. Kids are far more confident and challenging; they want to know everything and can prove your old wives' tales wrong with a Google search. They'll teach you how to use your new washing machine and know about the latest ruling against spanking in South Africa. Don't be surprised to hear about politics at the supper table, either.

What fascinates and sometimes frustrates me is how different each child is. It certainly is true when they say that each child comes with his or her own personality. As parents, we try to treat each one equally, and, in many respects, this works: equality in chores, in spending money, in play dates with friends and scoops of ice-cream on the weekend. But the emotional needs of each child are different and getting this right involves something of a learning process. The journey to helping your child achieve emotional wellbeing is one that will have you in bitter tears, filled with joy, wanting to pull your hair out and changing your perspective on life; all in a day.

I don't think our own parents were as in tune with emotional development. No one thought hard about how to phrase things, so that their child wouldn't be negatively impacted. "When I die then you'll know," was a common threat to lazy children in Indian households. Parents didn't hover around to see that their precious nugget wasn't bullied on the playground. Kids were much freer, then, and it helped make them more independent.

Today, turn to that same Google and you will be bombarded by parenting advice on every stage of your child's life, from toddler to teenager, and whether breast really is best. But no amount of research can properly prepare any parent.
Honestly, when I think of my three kids, they are worlds apart in personality and emotional needs. My eldest is a thinker and

a good sport. He is willing to try new things, reads books at a phenomenal rate and is naturally excellent in academics. This could be as a result of me spending loads of time reading to him, even when he was still in nappies.

My second and middle child is impulsive, a real live wire, witty and mischievous. He is resolute in his pursuit of sibling fairness and justice (usually because he gets scolded the most and rarely isn't the culprit). He is compassionate and has a kind heart but also determined to get what he wants, by all means necessary! Although it takes an immense amount of patience to deal with him and his homework, he has the potential to invent something life-changing if he puts his mind to it, or to become an advocate for a people that need him.

Then, my little girl, a premature baby, the child that receives the most attention. She is strong-willed and won't let an idea go. Her inquisitive mind often leaves me speechless. She is talkative and energetic, the apple of her father's eye. At seven years old, she is a determined little person, who, I hope, will one day become a leader for all the right reasons.

It's taken me a good few years to figure this parenting thing out and I still learn so much each day. The way I handle situations with my children changes from day to day. While sometimes I think I get it right, at other times I doubt myself. All I hope and pray for is that all of my children grow up to be well-rounded, emotionally secure individuals who know who they are and what they believe in – that they realise what their ultimate goal in life is and what they need to strive for. And I hope and pray that, in the end, I did a good enough job as a parent, so that I may also reap the rewards of raising kind, caring, thoughtful, non-judgemental and content human beings, who will contribute to the good in this world.

47 Porridge-brain syndrome
Feroza Arbee

As a mom of three kids (aged nine, six and two), I have been asked many times if porridge-brain syndrome exists. I am also a qualified medical specialist with several degrees. Let's consider that my intellectual baseline...

So, let me run you through a typical Saturday in my home...

It's a 'free' weekend, which means we (as a family) have not over-committed to social or academic events. There are no kids' sports training or tournaments to rush to and stand for hours on the side-lines, cheering, while keeping the littlies occupied and out of trouble. There are no school functions to set up, cater for or attend. There are no birthday parties to drop kids off at, while we socialise with parents we barely know. There are no visiting relatives to shop for, cook for or entertain. There are no workshops, conferences or seminars. It is just us...#bliss.

I decide to water the flowers and bushes that my kids planted weeks ago (my husband's attempt to make them more responsible and outdoorsy), once again forgotten and mom's responsibility. Besides, watering a garden is a mindful activity, isn't it?

The weekend is off to a good start!

As I dig the hose out from under the pile of toys and bicycles in the garage (mental note: must sort that out, the lady who collects for the orphanages messaged me last week), I look over at my dusty car and decide it could do with a good splash. As I walk towards the car with the keys to move it to the driveway, I notice washing on the line from yesterday (mental note: must speak to my helper). I put the keys on the pot-plant and take the washing to the ironing basket in the scullery. While there, I notice the dustbin is full. The garbage needs to be taken out. Since I'm going past the car to take the garbage out, I may as well put my shopping bags into the car in anticipation of my weekly shop later today. As I pick up the bags in the kitchen, I notice that the shopping list on my whiteboard seems incomplete. What have I been meaning to add on? Was it toilet paper? Nappies? What??

The kids, arguing in the kitchen, are not helping me think...

So I head to the bathroom to check. On the way, I find my daughter's show-and-tell on the floor. I pick it up to put it into her schoolbag for Monday. Before I get to her room, I see the TV remote lying on a chair. I pick it up because I know that all hell will break loose later, during much-awaited screen-time, when no one can find the remote. En route to the family room, I notice the water in the flower vase is murky and brown; I pick up the vase too. I spy my son's soccer togs under the dining room table. They've been there since Thursday! Mmm!! My not-so-mental note to speak to him is growled out under my breath.

By now my hands are full and I can't pick up anything else. I put everything down on the dining room table, a bit aggressively. The kids' argument in the kitchen has erupted into a Code 4 fight (a level which, I'm convinced, will cause my neighbours to call the police!). Yelling like a banshee, I break up the fight (they march in opposite directions and slam respective doors) and catch sight of my newly unpacked turquoise Le Creuset kettle (gifted to me) sitting decoratively on my hob. A cup of tea seems in order. It will help me relax and get to that mindful place...

As I sit on the patio (I made five mental notes while boiling the kettle) and enjoy my steaming cup in relative silence (the kids are temporarily sulking and the little one is standing outside their bedroom doors, begging them to let him in), I notice that the flower beds are dry and need watering...

It hits me like a tidal wave: I'm back where I started and the last hour has just been a 'busy' waste of time! I take several deep breaths and decide I really must make more effort to be mindful and relaxed...after I've done the shopping.

Where the hell are my car keys? I dig out the spare keys, while muttering irritably under my breath about being the only responsible person in the house who has to sort everything out. My husband wisely says that he'll watch the kids so that I can go to the mall by myself.

Who left the hose in the middle of the driveway?

As I enter the supermarket (it is crazy busy, I forgot its month-end), I realise I don't have my shopping list or bags. I don't know what we need, but I'll be damned if I waste a trip to the mall and arrive home empty-handed. I fill the trolley with stuff we don't need (peanut butter is on special; those plastic shoes look kind of cute, and let's not talk about the bakery section).

In a better mood, I unpack at home; only to realise we don't have milk, bread or bananas. I yell at the kids for not knowing where their show-and-tell or soccer togs are and for leaving them lying around. I feel guilty for yelling twice in one morning, so I order take-out for lunch, which makes me feel guiltier.

I stuff the empty take-out containers into the already-full dustbin. I'm stuck watching "PAW Patrol", because no one remembers where the remote is. The flower vase has dirty water and the flowers are dying. Am I the only one who sees these things? Am I the only one who cares?

I aggressively stuff the flowers into the overflowing bin. I yell at my family (they are used to it and calmly carry on watching "PAW Patrol" after mandatorily pretending to listen for a few seconds) and take myself off to the bathroom, my safe haven, the one place I can be guaranteed solitude and peace (the little one hasn't figured out how to open the door yet)...also the ideal place to make many mental notes.

My hysterical sobbing brings hubby to the door to ask hesitantly if I'm okay...I only manage to get three words out between sobs:

*NO*TOILET*PAPER*!!!

Sorry, what was the question again?

When the father is a better parent
Razina Theba

I thrive in a well-structured, predictable environment. So much so, that a psychometric assessment revealed that my personality was well-suited to a career in the military. I chose to study logical, reasonable and rule-bound law. Why would I marry a man whose idea of nirvana is to buy a subsistence farm and fish off the banks of his stream? This is my husband's idea of heaven. Sadly, he became a city advocate which put to bed any notions of waking up to farm-fresh life. We met at university. I attended all my lectures, while he sat under a Jacaranda tree lecturing his friends on the finer points of tying flies for fly-fishing.

He was not keen on us having children. There are already enough people on this earth, he told me. And besides, children come with their own personalities. "They are not as pliable as I am," he would tell me. "You may not get your way all the time". That should have been enough to put me off. I was undeterred and I was going to raise outstanding mini-versions of me. There is a book for everything, I told him. And there's Google.

My better half had foresight.

All unpredictable behaviour from either of my sons sent me sprinting to a book called, "Toddlers: The First Year," by the same authors of "What to Expect When You're Expecting." In the follow-up book, the "what to expect" part was clearly up for debate. My mother-in-law, who adores my sons but looks at my style of parenting with some ambivalence wryly remarked, "I don't know why you keep reading these books. They prey on the fact that you clearly have no idea what you are doing." Ouch!

The differences between my husband and me were amplified when we had children. My husband's style of parenting fluctuates between telling me to "relax" and telling the kids, "Listen to your mother," thereby pre-empting war.

When my son, Mikaeel, broke his arm at school, he looked me in the eye and said softly, "Phone Dad."

My son knows me well. The more anxious I get, the less helpful I become. "Is it sore? How sore? Does it feel broken? How broken? Do you need the loo? Rather just go to the loo before we go the hospital. On a scale of one to ten, how bad is it?"

He looked at me again, this time, desperate. "Please...Just... Call...Dad!"

Just as well I called. As we were getting Mikaeel into the car, broken elbow and everything, in my haste to be the good mother I slammed the car door into his broken arm. Father and son had a *mashwara* about whether or not I should even go with them to the hospital. Muttering under their breaths, they begrudgingly agreed that I could, on condition that I did not say or touch anything.

My husband is, without a doubt, the better parent. He is also the more popular parent. He instinctively knows my sons' needs. I have never said to my kids, "Wait until your father gets home." In fact, they look forward to him vindicating them.

Before I became a mother I would look at children who had cavities disdainfully. How negligent can a mother be? "Make brushing teeth non-negotiable," I would think to myself. Nothing would prepare me for how I would grovel and implore my own children to brush their teeth. I naively thought that I had won that battle until the dentist told me that my son had nine cavities. That week, I could be heard muttering to myself, "nine, nine, nine, nine". To this day, the number nine holds negative significance for me. My husband's expectations were much lower. He was so proud that his son allowed a dentist to look into his mouth without the dentist being injured. (People who rely on their digits avoid my children; the last hairdresser had to have five stitches sewn between her index finger and thumb.)

Part of my madness as a mother was my emphasis on reading. I was the Patron Saint and my son the worthy cause. And read I did. I started reading to him when he was two months old, and not just kids' books. Instructions to car seat adjustments, recipes for malva pudding and even dry cleaning tags were part of my repertoire. Mikaeel is now eleven and he despises the printed word.

Germs were another source of angst for me. I sterilised my babies' bottles until they were two years old. My kids knew never to touch buttons on a lift or hold arm rails. "Those never get wiped," I would warn them. On one outing to a pizza place I noticed that my then four-year old was unusually quiet. As I chatted to friends, he emerged from under the table chewing a massive amount of food. It took me a moment to realise that our food had not arrived. After prying his mouth open, I found an assortment of gum that other patrons had stuck to the bottom of the table. With surgeon-like precision and a well-developed pincer grip, he had managed to dislodge all of it. Stimorol, Clorets, Airwaves. The overriding smell was Purple Chicks. I pinned him down to the floor, WWF style, straddled his little body and extracted the last of the gum.

I cannot be anything but dramatic on an ordinary day, but on this day I was exceptional. My rant to his dad was magnificent. His response was incredulous, "They still make Purple Chicks? Mikaeel, how were those PURPLE ones?" I juggled thoughts of unmentionable, unpronounceable diseases, and yet nobody was worse for wear. It was also the year my son did not have a single cough or cold.

I often worry about my sons being raised in a home with no sisters. Will they value women? Are we raising sons with a social conscience? I asked my younger son, Amaan, my ray of sunshine, to write a Mother's Day card for my mother. With the sure-footedness of a mountain goat that only an eight-year-old could possess, he wrote, "Dearest *Naani*, you (are) the buzz of the bees in my heart. And you cook *biryani* for me and I know it is full of love."

It is undeniably worth it. There are just no rules, and I am learning to live with that.

Pearls of wisdom

Until you have children, you will not know how capable you are of deeply loving another human being. This old adage is absolutely true. **Razina Theba**

Intimacy plays an important part in marriage and inevitably (in most cases) kids come with that. Make space for a third person in the relationship and for its effects on intimacy. **Maymoonah Chohan**

Be open to exploring your body and your reactions to different stimuli. Once you know your preferences, advise your spouse. Sex is a beautiful way to express and deepen love between each other. It's new for the couple and rather than letting each other guess, advise what is pleasurable or unacceptable. **Raashida Khan**

If both people are committed to mutual love, respect, kindness and compassion, it helps to sooth 'teething problems'. **Afzad-Al**

Keep what happens in the bedroom, in the bedroom. Never allow anyone into this sacred and private domain. **Somayya Hansrod**

If you are experiencing difficulty being intimate with your husband, speak to a health care provider. There is a solution to every problem. **Anonymous**

Do your Kegels. Kegel exercises strengthen the pelvic floor muscles, which support the uterus, bladder, small intestine and rectum. Though Kegel exercises don't actually tighten your vagina, they tone and strengthen your vaginal muscles, boosting your arousal, thus making intercourse easier. **Anonymous**

THE SELF-ESTEEM OF A MUSLIM WOMAN

My sense of self was so integrally tied to other people's opinions of me that I have had to dig really deeply to find my authenticity and allow it to shine, irrespective of what others may think or feel. How did I expect someone to know me, love me when I did not know me or love me?

Rehana Moosajee

Letter to my daughter
Rehana Moosajee

25 August 2017

My beautiful darling daughter – Faheemah

Earlier this month you turned twenty and I am now 47. This letter is my attempt to share with you lessons I have learnt in the hope that, as you journey through life, make your own mistakes, register your own victories and learn your own lessons – some of my story can be a reference point for you. You can choose to take what serves you and disregard what does not – for no two people are replicas of each other's lives.

At your age I was so much more naive than you are. I truly believed in the notion of a happily-ever-after marriage and the sense that I was in some way incomplete until a husband came and fulfilled me. Looking back, I realise just how little sense of self I had when, at age 21, against the advice of many people, I married the boy I had been romantically involved with since I was 16. It felt like a Romeo and Juliet type relationship – his family certainly did not approve of me, but came to propose and there was big wedding that was totally different from anything I would have planned.

You can imagine my shock, heartbreak and anguish when, just over a year later, I was divorced. I have struggled for a long time to understand what the cause of that divorce actually was, and it was many things. But (mostly from my perspective, now) marriage was a way for him to rebel against what his family stood for by marrying a girl that was considered an outsider in every way. Once he had me, he grew bored and started telling me how he and his parents felt he should rather be married to someone in his family.

I liked to think of myself as a really strong woman, and so, rather than crying and allowing myself to feel the deep pain and anguish, I chose to bury it and continue with life. A trip to the United Kingdom, a wonderful teaching career and being introduced to your father two months after my *iddat* were all sufficiently exciting and distracting to allow me to hide from my pain.

In your father I saw a worldly-wise man, ten years older than me, a traveller with a lot of tales and a political activist who took a stand against poverty and injustice and had deep compassion for other human beings. My attraction was based very much on my own neediness for a knight in shining armour who would come and rescue me from my previous heartache. I now know that we all carry our own deep wounds from the multiplicity of relationships we have before we meet our spouse. Nobody can take away the pain of another. Solace comes from going deep within, turning to your Creator, and – a lesson I have learnt only recently – sitting with your pain and feeling your way through it.

We live in a society and culture that prizes the marital relationship above all others. Yet, we have numerous relationships before we meet our life partner. Each relationship creates an imprint on our heart, which shapes how we relate in marriage. The most important relationships that should be cultivated from birth are with God (Allah/Creator) and with oneself. I entered into two marriages with no self-love, making it the responsibility of another to love me, when I really did not know or love myself.

The greatest gift that your father has given me in our marriage is the space to work through my own confusion about my identity. My sense of self was so integrally tied to other people's opinions of me that I have had to dig really deeply to find my authenticity and allow it to shine, irrespective of what others may think or feel. How did I expect someone to know me, love me when I did not know me or love me? In many ways, I have been my own biggest critic – never able to love myself unconditionally, always needing to prove myself and wait for acclaim and acknowledgement to come from outside.

The role that your father has played has not been at all easy. In my deepest anguish after yet another one of our altercations and arguments, many of which you have been witness to, when accusations have pierced through me and my tears have flooded on my *musallah*, I have had to reconnect with my heart – the one that I closed for fear it would be hurt again. It is no wonder that I have found deep comfort in the saying, "It is only in the remembrance of Allah that hearts find satisfaction".

It has taken me a really long time to fathom that, when you numb yourself to feeling for fear of being hurt again, you cheat the world of your gifts. I had closed off my beautiful, pure heart many years ago, and, with each subsequent hurt, I sealed it off even more. The process of opening it is still underway, but, my daughter, in life you are meant to learn to navigate many emotions and I would encourage you to feel them all, because the alternative is existence, not life. Embrace the challenges and the pain, because they serve to stretch your soul and make you grow.

In an age where separation and divorce are the default position, and walking out of a marriage has become the fashionable thing to do, it is a lot wiser – albeit more painful – to work through your issues. Financial independence and careers make it a lot easier for women of my generation and yours to leave a marriage, than it was for our grandmothers. But leaving a marriage does not mean you have resolved your deep-seated issues. Sometimes, our marriage partners are the mirrors that hold up to us the ways in which we treat ourselves. I am not advocating that you endure pain, suffering and injustice in a marriage, but my life has taught me that you cannot change another person. If you want to change your life, you need to start with yourself.

Two marriages and many painful lessons later, I can recall painful scenes as if they just happened yesterday; the hurtful things that were said or done, my deep pain when my intentions and motivations were misunderstood. All of these have led me to the deepest recesses of my heart, a place I know my Creator has access to. He knows my life story, the heart-wrenching choices that have shaped me and the intention behind the things I have said or done.

So, my darling daughter, as you move through life, I leave you with these words:

a. Know yourself.
b. A wedding and a marriage are two different things – focus on the latter not the former.

c. Your partner has relationships with parents, siblings, family that pre-date your arrival in his life, in the same way that you do. Nurture each relationship that is important to you and give him the space to do the same.

d. Nobody is perfect; we all have our own fears and issues. Learn to listen from a place of compassion, with an open-heart; not with judgement and the need to impose your own views.

e. Those who, rather than agreeing with all you say, give you advice in ways that challenge you, taking you outside of your comfort zone, truly care about you.

I have no idea where your life will take you regarding marriage and relationships. For me, whilst so many other aspects of my life have been relatively easy, marriage and relationships have been the source of my deepest learning about myself, the world and the stepping stone to my relationship with my Creator.

I love you.

Mummy

It's all about your mind-set...
Fatima Kazee

Life is pretty much a series of expectations. We expect to experience something in a certain way, based on what we perceive it to be, only to realise that it is nothing like that. Marriage, for me, is like that on an ongoing basis. In the beginning, the love and adoration you feel for your spouse is so overwhelming that it's almost impossible to imagine anything less than a perfect fairy tale. I distinctly recall daydreams of sun-kissed days, cookbook quality meals, romantic evenings at the fireplace, sweet, faultless offspring to complete a picket-fenced home, and waking up every morning to a smooth, relaxed day, ending in dessert that never makes me put on any unwanted weight. What I've learnt along the way, in all aspects of my life is that what you bring in with you, together with your mind-set, determines how things pan out. The same rings true for marriage.

Every person has a different upbringing and childhood. Take my personal story as an example – I came from what could be called a 'disrupted' home; my parents got divorced when I was a young child. Their divorce affected me. Even prior to their separation, I remember being shrouded in a dark cloud. I always felt stressed and uneasy. I have since learnt that this was the beginning of the anxiety I live with.

My husband, in comparison, is a 'whole' person; a well-rounded individual who grew up with feelings of warmth, caring, support, guidance and love. Don't get me wrong, not a day in my mother's hardworking life did she not love me. She always considered my brother and me before herself. Priorities and focus were on making ends meet and raising good kids.

But I believe that divorce can compromise children's emotional integrity and wellbeing. No doubt, a child missing the father or mother will need more attention and nurturing; a catch-22 situation, because, inevitably, the parent will have issues of their own to deal with. Important milestones, such as matriculation, graduation, getting married, having a child of their own are examples of times when a child will feel disappointed when one parent cannot be or simply is not present.

I remember that, when I discovered I was pregnant with my first child, I felt shocked, unprepared and bewildered by what was to come. I was upset, and with good reason – I still hadn't completed my law articles and all my plans were now compromised.

Thankfully, I had a really easy pregnancy, but my birth experience was terrifying. I spent two days in labour before I gave birth to a beautiful but colicky baby. The nightmare! I didn't even know that a baby needed to be winded each time he drank and that he needed a change of nappy, too. I was ill-prepared, sleep deprived and milk-laden to the point of immense pain. It took me a long time to come to terms with having a child of my own and I felt permanently guilt-ridden. I guessed that other mothers didn't feel this way at all, which made things worse. I had so much to think about. Would I complete my articles? Would I continue working? My mind was in constant turmoil with new thoughts and worries.

My husband, on the other hand, had a magic touch. He had a patient and effortless way about everything he did with our baby. Even both grannies were calm and soothing to the little guy.

So, reconciling how I felt and dealt with situations in my life, as compared to my husband, was and is difficult. It is almost as if we are from two opposite worlds. I reside in chaos and irrational anxiety. My husband is always calm, caring and reasonable.

My life is a marathon, with me the runner. I want to finish the race but the course is exhausting, and I don't think that I've trained enough for it. I can't be a failure, not to myself and not to the people who mean the most to me. I can't and I won't give up.

What comes as baggage from dysfunction is a range of anxiety, low self-esteem, self-doubt, and a need for constant approval. Sometimes showing and accepting love is difficult, perhaps people become weary or afraid of the possibility of being let down or feeling vulnerable again. Or afraid of being happy because, inevitably, it ends in sadness...doesn't it?

I can't expect anyone to understand what my journey has been like. But holding onto that journey, to that past, always blaming and raising 'that' defence is exactly what will break everything. My husband taught me that valuable lesson and it took me a good few years to acknowledge and own it. I am always the more emotional, feisty and temperamental one.

He is always reasonable, rational and level-headed. He has helped me to change my mind-set: my perspective on life and how I react to situations. ("It's not what you say, it's how you say it," he says.)

Even when it comes to matters of religion, we had completely differing takes on what being a Muslim should be. On my end, it was rather negative (as was most of my outlook on life) and fearful, with all the consequences of non-compliance guiding me to fulfil my Islamic duties. His version was a perfect blend of mercy, peace, forgiveness, love and light.

In essence, the way I look at it now, we are perfectly paired – opposite in every way! He loves the bush, I love being at home. He has patience with our three kids; I bring the house down when I find soccer boots lying in the lounge. I can live on toasted cheese forever; he loves good food. Together, we provide our children with what they need. Because, from my personal experience, parents are the mirror to their children – compassion, kindness, understanding, humility, good values and loads of laughs – that's what makes for a good marriage and a 'perfect' family.

The fairest of us all
Yasmin Denat

"Indeed the most noble of you in the sight of Allah is the righteous of you."
(Quran; chapter 49, *Surah* Al Hujaraat / The Chambers – verse 13)

From what I remember, I was the proverbial ugly duckling – completely devoid of the grace of a swan or the agility and finesse of an eagle. For the greater part, I would have been absolutely delighted to be one of those common brown garden finches that wander around largely unnoticed, blending seamlessly into their surroundings.

I was a small-framed girl; short would probably be one of the first adjectives people would use to describe me. But there was another crucial element to my existence: from as far back as I can remember, I have had chronic eczema. As a young child, I was predominantly unaffected by the aesthetics of my affliction, this was due to the unwavering love and support of my parents. I was never taught to cover up or be ashamed of "the dreaded rash", as we called it.

For me as a young child, the eczema was mainly about the discomfort – constant dryness, burning and itching. I didn't realise that it had such a negative visual impact; I didn't see it as people saw it. I remained an introverted, yet happy child, immersed in the comfort of my own company and my love of books and the written word. During my schooling years, I finally began seeing myself as I perceived others to see me.

Most kids have some sort of self-esteem issues as they grow up and enter their teens, but having a visible skin disease raises the insecurities of a teenage girl to an entirely new level. There are innumerable factors that lead to the destruction of self-esteem in adolescents: being chunky, skinny, hairy or having acne all determine whether you are cool or not. Being accepted is a major component of growing up, and the craving for acceptance is at the core of teenagers being affected by peer pressure. Thankfully, I did not become a victim of peer pressure in any major way.

The 1990s was a gentler, more accepting era in my life, and my love of reading and a small group of friends were ample to sustain me. I didn't want to be noticed any more than necessary, and my main objective, whenever I was in a new social setting, was to fade into the background, hoping people wouldn't notice the blotches, redness and scaling on my skin.

I also resented being called cute because I was short; I didn't want to be a stereotypical girl who loved pink, shiny things and I loathed the thought of becoming a 'Barbie'-like figure. I chose for myself a serious, intellectual persona, and my passion for reading became my escape and means of growth. Throughout this period, I was self-conscious and kept my circle small. I definitely still craved some acceptance but I would never have defined myself as an individual who lacked self-esteem.

My later teenage years were slightly different; I had a few solid friends and a greater sense of self, which lead to a greater degree of confidence. I had morphed substantially during that phase; subconsciously I had decided to be more assertive, opinionated and vocal. Suddenly, I knew what I wanted and I where I wanted to go. I grew comfortable in my own skin, so to speak. I steered clear of being the popular princess type, and, even though I wouldn't admit it then, it was because of my learnt insecurities. It's a simple survival tool: focus on your strengths and hide or ignore your weakness.

Throughout this period, apart from the few compulsory actions and the religious instruction I received daily at *madressah*, Islam played a minor role in the development of my identity. I did not consider it to be central part of my being. I was never compelled to dress modestly or to follow an Islamic lifestyle, although I could quite easily have chosen to do so. But I chose otherwise; I wholeheartedly subscribed to the typically secular picture of success. I wanted to go to university, get a degree and have a career. In the interim, I had also fallen hopelessly in love, so I decided to add marriage to my plans.

So, in a short timespan I achieved it all: the degree, the job, the marriage – but in the end, apart from my marriage, these achievements brought me little joy. The stress of moving to a new city took me completely out of my comfort zone and had devastating effects on my health. My eczema was the worst it had ever been in my life; weeping, red, angry patches that caused me great pain and even greater embarrassment and my hair fell out in clumps. I started hating myself, getting depressed and moody. To the outside world I had succeeded, but this did nothing to improve my state of mind.

I started judging myself, my work suffered, my marriage suffered and my self-esteem started to deteriorate. Every day was an endless vortex of nothingness. I hated my body, my skin; even intimacy felt like a chore. If it wasn't for the emotional strength of my spouse and his unconditional support, I probably would have fallen into a far worse state. He kept turning my attention to Allah.

When I left the corporate world, I finally felt as if I could breathe again. I went back to studying, and, even though being a mother scared me and was not in my plans, I fell pregnant. But I finally began to see the bigger picture: all of this was part of a divine plan, and as a result, my relationship with Allah finally began to develop.

It was only when I stopped judging myself according to society's standards that my health and state of mind improved. Self-esteem determines how you carry yourself and interact with those around you, and so, as I made peace with my impending motherhood and implemented some personal reforms and a greater adherence to my faith, I started seeing myself in a more positive light. As I grew, my marriage grew, my faith grew and my sense of self grew. I finally felt confident again, and the less I focused on my eczema, the more it seemed to heal.

My baby added a whole new dimension to my life; my aspirations became less focused on what I thought society expected of me and more on the peace and happiness of my own family. Each subsequent child came with a whole new set of challenges, but each I time I grew and developed new strengths. My family gave me purpose. The more I reflected on my life, the more content I felt; the more I submitted to Allah and his will, the more obedient I was to his law, the better I felt. I started valuing myself as Allah values us, according to our *imaan* which is the paramount value of a human being.

The value and respect given to Muslim women gave me great pride. As I read about the business prowess of *Hadrat* Khadija and the scholarly nature of *Hadrat* Aaisha, my zeal to become a better Muslim grew, as well. Gone was my fascination with Simone de Beauvoir and Frida Kahlo. Muslim women were warriors and academics; they were entrepreneurs and heroines – why had I denied myself my true identity? I was from the nation of Prophet Muhammed (PBUH), I was a Muslim woman: I embraced it and redefined myself according to divine values. This gave me a deep sense of inner peace. It was something I was going to teach my daughters, to be proud Muslim women; to realise that the Disney princess was not the epitome of perfection.

The crowning moment for me came when I decided to cover my face and wear the *niqab*. Deciding to do this was mammoth, but once I did it, I felt a great sense of power. Finally, I had decided to stop encountering life via pre-determined social constructs. The world would see me only as I chose to be seen, guarding my modesty and donning the *hijab* and *niqab*. The very things I had once seen as orthodox had given me power.

It's a cruel and fast-paced world indeed, a world where aesthetics has taken on the greatest role and society has given appearances more value than ever before in history. It's a tough time to be growing up or even growing old; everything is digitally recorded and exposed. It's no wonder that personal insecurities have peaked and depression rates are soaring. People live to update their status on social media platforms.

We have become a species who travel not to experience, but to view the world from behind a lens, who prepare food to look at, who raise children that appear happy. Somewhere along the way we have dismally lost the essence of our being, the essence of living. Our definition of self-esteem has become dependent on social constructs of beauty and associated norms.

On my travels over the past few years I have become aware that the subjective, western notions of perfect beauty and body shape are far from universal. The more we seek to align ourselves with divine values, the less we will be concerned about these images and classifications. Once superficial constructs fall away, a person can truly focus on self-reformation, an arduous journey for me and one that will be perpetual.

Prophet Muhammed (PBUH) narrates: "Surely Allah does not look towards your form or your wealth, but he looks towards your hearts and your deeds." (Sahih Muslim, 2564)

Finding myself in my marriage
Maimoonah Gori

For me, marriage is like a delightful meal that takes much thought, energy, time, patience, and practice to perfect. The adding of aromatic and magical spices that merge together creates that beautiful bond, which stands the test of time.

My marriage started off beautifully, with everything new: new beddings, new dishes, new furniture, new surname and a new partner; that's why we use the term 'new beginnings'. Like many brides, I was in a euphoric state for a long time. I adapted easily into my new life, taking things in my stride, but as the days passed, I realised that I did things differently.

The transition from a Miss to a Mrs takes some time to digest. Within a month into marriage, there is such a dramatic change – from young carefree girl to wife. Our expectations crack when we have self-doubt and are tested in our marriage.

My thoughts and ideas sometimes differed from those of my partner or his family, but I had to fit in. That was challenging, as I was still finding myself in my marriage. But I followed the routine and did what was expected of me. As I was new, I had to adapt to their house and rules, which I respected. Their household was the complete opposite of mine, and, although I had my own place, on weekends and holidays I was at my in-laws. Thanks to my mother, who taught me to how be flexible, I managed; otherwise, I would have been a nervous wreck. Her golden advice was, "Respect, stay silent, and don't carry tales from one to another".

How do you adapt to a house full of people and children? We always had people over, but this was different. It is very difficult to open up overnight and become buddies with your in-laws. These are new people, the common bond is your husband. Although I was grateful to my husband, who supported me, the feeling of loneliness and my love for my parents and family washed over me from time to time.

At that time I was a student on campus, and I did not fit the daughter-in-law mould. At times, I had a feeling that I was becoming someone I wasn't and I battled to find myself, but I had to fit in and learn.

I have a very good built-in mechanism: whenever I have a self-doubt, I talk myself out of it, crushing it with some logic. At the time, I also spoke to my husband, and sometimes he managed to quell it. My mind-set was very positive, so I subconsciously become 'deaf' if someone dropped a hint about my cooking skills, or if I did something different. I was determined to make my marriage work, and was not prepared to get involved in gossip or currying favours from one sister-in-law or another. At first, it was hard, as I didn't know when a family member was being sincere or when they just wanted some information that I might unconsciously give. I was the outsider, and any wrong move from me would either end in an argument or cause stress in my marriage. I was so busy with my studies and my home; there was no time for trivial stuff.

I was new in the kitchen and very eager to prepare meals and try out new ideas, but some things only come right after years of practice and patience. Sometimes, my husband would unconsciously tell me, "It was nice, but something was missing." I would be upset and overreact, making it into an argument. Then I would feel miserable. Some days I was in tears, other days upset over trivial issues. But we women are creatures of emotion; we respond to everything emotionally. With time and patience, I learnt that I had to please someone else besides me; just as I liked things a certain way, so did my partner. We were two different people, with two different temperaments.

Come motherhood: now that drives any woman insane. Our bodies have a mind of their own, clothes don't fit, everything gets bigger. My poor husband had to take my grumpiness, mood swings and frustration in his stride.

Once baby arrives, the sleepless nights and the juggling that goes with being a mother take a toll on the body and emotions. With it comes wishing we were still slim, smarter, better; all these thoughts eating at our self-esteem. I was like a roller coaster: emotional, hungry and unhappy with the extra weight gain.

As days passed, I learnt to adjust, accept the changes, move on and be happy. The main thing in marriage is the moving on, and making it work. This means creating a beautiful environment where the family is happy, and understanding the needs of your children and partner. Having six children did not stop me from being a mother and a woman, in fact it has boosted me and allowed me to find myself. How?

I find peace of mind and heart in prayer.
I accept what I have been blessed with: my family and friends.
I appreciate what my husband and children do for me.
I say "thank you" every day, to show I care.
I love my partner unconditionally; come what may, we stand together.
I remain positive, seeing good in everything, but if something is not right I am assertive.
I always forgive and bear no grudges: only then can you move on.

The way we speak to ourselves internally affects how we feel, so it is important to love ourselves first. If we love ourselves first, then we can love those around us. As the years move on, so does marriage. You and your partner learn to understand each other and complement each other. In the end, it's you and your soulmate loving each other unconditionally, respecting the other and bringing out the best in each other.

Writing my own script
Shaakira Rahiman-Saleh

Gentle hues of a subdued orange-painted landscape filter into our lounge. Giggles and mischief interrupt and fill the evening air. Ignoring the jumping on my ivory leather lounge suite (a choice a mother of three should never have made), I crave to join in the laughter. Somehow I manage to keep my focused 'mother face' on, although I am increasingly tempted to just let go and set my inner child free. I remind myself: "There are just too many things to get done, and it's almost supper time!"

EEEK! I dash into the kitchen and begin to slice a cucumber; the hastened chopping against my wooden board is unapologetically noisy. This is my last-minute attempt to add something healthy to the delicious *ghee*-laden curry and rice about to grace my already-set dining room table.

This scene is as I had always imagined it and more, my very own perfect 'happy family setting' I spent most of my younger years dreaming about. It is not the 'ultra-perfect' kind you see on social media and so-called reality shows. There are no staged smiles placed in opulent settings, no 'keeping up with the

Kardashians'. Rather picture this: toys strewn all about the floor, the whole lot of us already in our pyjamas, far too early in the evening. My youngest boy, four-year-old Muhammad Bilal sports dishevelled hair and missing socks from playful pillow fights and what may have been a more intense cat fight this evening amongst siblings (amusingly also involving our cat, Poppy, who is convinced she is one of the children).

As I listen to my family's banter, I realise how much this means to me. While chopping the greens, I reflect deeply on my life – reaching my thirties and my first decade of being married (all praise be to Allah) – and it occurs to me that slicing my fingers is a strong possibility. I am privileged to be a modern-day South African Muslim woman who exercises her right to pursue her dreams and fulfil her career, whilst also being a committed full-time mother and wife.

I shudder to think about Muslim women who are under the current barbaric Isis, Mossad or Boko Haram regimes; those who have suffered for decades before these new groups were even created; and also those women closer to home who remain oppressed by the so-called banner of religion – a cowardly excuse used by some men as a means of control, with no understanding of the true religion of peace and equality and also, very disturbingly, who have neither love for nor fear of their Creator.

Alhamdulillah, I am fortunate and blessed to have a kind, understanding and patient husband (may Allah always keep him that way).

"Is supper ready yet?" Zuber enquires from down the passage as he makes his to the kitchen.

"Just a minute or two, baby," I reply unconvincingly.

He smiles, knowing I actually mean twenty minutes. "Okay, I'm going to relax for a bit. Let me know when we are ready to eat."

Zuber, as passive as he is, has always stood up for what is right and is not afraid to admit when he (or I, mind you) is wrong and things need to change. I am truly thankful for a husband who is always present, willing and happy to give and receive love; qualities that are very hard to find in today's techno-obsessed, semi-present and antisocial world.

Zuber is fully involved in most aspects of our children's upbringing. This evening, all phones and devices on charge and behind closed doors, he helps the kids wash their hands and begins the meal with a *duah*. As I say "Aameen", we smile to each other, amused as the children compete over which pieces of meat they call dibs on. I begin to dish out the steaming aromatic rice.

"This is the new brown basmati rice we bought the other day," I confirm to Zuber as I dish out. He is most enthusiastic about a healthy meal plan to accompany his new gym programme this week (I hope he won't notice my heavy-handedness with the *ghee*).

As I dish out, I think to myself that, of all the things I have learnt to appreciate about Zuber in these ten years, is that he supports and encourages my freedom to choose. We have always thought of our union as a team and he has never been an authoritative, dominating figure in the household. Not to say that he always agrees with me, we have our fair share of differences and at times unpleasant fights. But we have at these times learnt to agree to disagree, giving each other space and a fair chance to consider the other side of the argument, seek wise counsel, and, most importantly, put our trust in Allah. I have never been let down by Him.

I hope I will never take for granted this gift of choice and the space to consciously write my own script on a daily basis. I emphasise this point because, with many things in life, I have not had a choice. I did not have the choice to grow up in a 'normal' nuclear family, like most of my friends and classmates. I did not choose how I came into this world – I was born 'a mistake' – although I have been shunned for it. I was not responsible for the choices my parents made, although I had to live through the repercussions and shame.

Anyone who has grown up in a similar setting to mine, who didn't know one or both of their parents, painfully experienced their parents' divorce, had a parent consciously choose not to be a part of their life, or had a parent who was physically there but who, in fact, was truly 'absent' will know how this creates a feeling of emptiness inside, a void that just cannot be filled. Personally, my biggest heartache and test in life was my own mother leaving me, without a good enough reason for a five-year-old to understand. My mother embodied everything I knew that was safe and beautiful, and then...I learnt the truth of my existence. And the choices my father made broke my heart before any boy could.

Living through all the difficult experiences that surrounded my childhood was not my choice. But I live this truth and I accept what Allah has decreed for me, because, through the hurt, I have found countless blessings.

I have realised that Allah doesn't always give you what you want in the way you expect it, but what you need in a way necessary for you to grow, to learn and to fulfil your own unique destiny. I may not have had my biological parents at my side, but I have had more than one mother and father and received more love than many children do. (The converse, however, is also true: as a teenager, it seemed to me that I also endured triple the shouting and flack when I stumbled or did something wrong.) As I remember those who shaped and moulded my life, I am overwhelmed with emotion, especially for those who have passed on. My eldest daughter, Asma, a six-year-old young lady, notices the tears swelling up. She stops eating and asks me softly, "What's wrong Mama?"

"Nothing my angel," I reply, "I just miss my Aunty Rashida who made the best curry and rice I've ever tasted."

I have learnt that Allah takes care of you. I marvel at how I grew up in a home where my aged and frail *Naani* took care of me during weekdays and over weekends, while my mother and Aunty Rashida sold jewellery at the flea market to get by. From humble beginnings, *Alhamdullah*, I attended a private school, graduated in the field and university of my choice without loans or begging, paid for my own first car and financed my own wedding.

The whispers always haunted me: "She will never find a decent Muslim man or family, knowing that she comes from a broken home." With the grace of Allah, I married into a large, traditional and well-respected Saleh family. My husband always reassures me that he is proud of me and married me for who I am and not my past, which I had no control over. I am often consoled and reflect on what is so beautifully written in the Quran: "Allah does not burden a soul beyond that it can bear" (*Surah* 2, Verse 286). I believe that it is only Allah who has looked after me through kind people, jobs I have been fortunate to earn and my own initiative.

Don't let what is out of your control stop you from doing what is in your control. Sometimes we are so focused on the negative aspects of a situation or our lives in general, that it hinders us from doing what is actually in our control. Don't allow yourself to feel despondent and become oblivious to the fact that you can somehow change the situation for the better. I believe nothing is impossible or hopeless, and Allah has given each one of us everything that is needed to lead a happy and contented life, we just need to choose to.

I spent most of my teenage years depressed, wondering why my mother hadn't had an abortion. In those years, having a baby before marriage was much more of scandal than it is today. I felt that I had brought shame on my family; that I was a burden thrust upon my Aunt Rashida and my Uncle Rafiq and Aunty Fazila – although they never tried to make me feel this way. *Alhamdulillah* for these angels Allah has put on my path. But in my youth I often felt hopeless and questioned the reason for my existence.

Life felt meaningless at times, especially after enduring the losses of, first, *Naani* Khatija, who passed away when I was four; then my mother, who left when I was five; and then my pillar of strength, Aunty Rashida, who passed away when I was sixteen. It took me almost thirty years to realise that things don't have to be perfect, to be happy. Happiness is not an achievement, but rather a choice you can make for yourself.

"But Mummy, you make the best food, ever!" says little Nusaybah, in her attempt to make me feel better.

Her older brother and sister chime in, "Yes, you do, mama, we love you. Don't cry, mama".

As I look at their cute, yet wary faces, I make light of the situation, telling them that I haven't reached the ranks of all their *naanis* or their *daadis* in the kitchen just yet, and I get up to give each one a squeeze, to reassure them that everything is fine.

Life may have its ups and downs, but at this very moment it is perfect. It is exactly where I am destined to be and I accept it for all the blessings and the challenges it presents. I believe Allah wants us to be happy, even though at times we wonder why are we tested so much and we feel distraught, helpless, weak and alone. But no matter what, we are always capable of doing something; whether we change the situation for the better or change the way we view the situation.

My advice is never to take the power and freedom of choice for granted. And, is it not beautiful to know that before Allah joined the waters and the sands, He wrote our names next to our partners', and out of His bounty graced us with the choice of whether to have them or not? I am grateful that He guided me to make this choice.

Love lost and found
Waasila Jassat

I have a story to tell. I fell in love with a good man and got married at age 26. A year later we had a bouncy baby boy. A year later the marriage was over...

That is not the story though. I won't be telling a sweet story of romance or a tragic tale of a bitter divorce. I won't be sharing funny anecdotes or heart-breaking moments of despair. You won't hear of the heroes and villains in this tale. Those details belong in the sanctity of a marriage, protected by sincere vows, regardless of the way the relationship ended.

This story starts when I found myself a young(ish) single mother of a little toddler.

Suddenly I was alone, experiencing a profound sense of loss. Loss, not only of a person who had been a huge part of my life, but loss of the life that we had, and the promise of a future we could have had. I experienced a feeling of having failed: what went wrong and what could I have done differently? And I felt shame: how embarrassing – we had that lovely big wedding...

The negativity I felt did not last long, but I did allow those feelings to surface, play in my mind and then settle. I was determined not to be weighed down with hatred and regret. I made a conscious choice to forgive him and forgive myself and I welcomed and encouraged him to be a part of his son's life. It did help that he lived halfway across the world – an important factor for a happy divorce!

I allowed myself to grieve a little, then picked myself up and got on with things. I am grateful for two things at that point. I had a loving and supportive family who embraced me with kindness, unquestioning loyalty and zero judgement. I had an education, resources, means and abilities at my disposal. I worked, and, *Alhamdulillah*, I could earn my keep, so I wasn't a burden on my parents and didn't require support from my ex.

The next few years were a period of great personal growth. I made a happy home for my family of two. I set out to improve myself. I wanted to further my studies, so that I would be better able to apply my mind and my skills. I wanted to be financially independent, so I could live free of debt. Most importantly, I wanted to be a better version of me. I spent time thinking about my life, my goals, my priorities. As Socrates once said, "An unexamined life is not worth living". I did the difficult thing of looking in the mirror, confronting what I didn't like and taking steps to be better. *Shukr*, out of this process I experienced a spiritual awakening, started to realise the purpose of my existence and made a firm resolution to be a better human being, to contribute to the world around me.

As far as practical realities go, I bought a home, dealt with renovations, sorted out repairs, paid the bills, planned holidays. Yes, I did all these things myself, because I had to, and I managed. But I had a lot of help. I learnt the truth in the

African proverb, "It takes a village to raise a child". I was blessed and remain eternally grateful for the family, friends and neighbours who helped me – babysitting when I had to travel, cooking a meal when I ran late at work, offering lift clubs and play dates when I had too much on my plate, inviting us on holidays so we always felt included. In this way, many full and happy years passed by. It wasn't the traditional nuclear family but it was 'our normal' and we made it work. I learnt there is no perfect family or home. People find happiness in whatever circumstances they are in.

And now, it seems, in the blink of an eye, I have reached age 40. I feel I have lived a full life – I married, divorced, raised a kid, studied, studied some more, travelled to many places, lived in a different city for a while, lived in a different country for while...Along the way, I have accumulated memories, experiences and deep friendships. At 40 I have paused to reflect and take stock, and I reckon I've earned the right to share my experience, impart some wisdom, and, heck (why not!), even to preach a little.

Just to be clear, I won't give lessons on being the perfect wife, mother or daughter-in-law. That's a different chapter, not written by me. I can't tell you how to be the perfect host of afternoon tea, delighting all who attend with tasteful décor and patisserie, but around my dining table we do share hearty meals and belly aching laughter.

I don't post the meals I cook on Instagram, because in my home (after saying *bismillah*) we eat all the food before we can whip out our smartphones.

I don't make round *rotis* or any other shape of *rotis*, but I do know where to buy them and I heat them up perfectly.

My freezers are not stacked with savoury stockpiles a month before *Ramadaan*, instead we eat simply most days and enjoy all those yummy things when we are invited to *naani*, aunties, cousins and friends.

I don't pack amazing school lunches of salmon-stuffed croissants, and thankfully my son prefers a classic cheese sandwich and a few variations on this.

My boy hasn't attended kumon mathematics centres, UCMAS brain development programmes or horse-riding lessons, and he hasn't learnt to speak Chinese or play the violin, but he has tons of free time to chill, play soccer and hang out with his friends – and he's quite a cool, funny and well-adjusted kid.

I don't follow the latest *hijab* trends and YouTube tutorials; I have two different *hijab* styles and they each take five seconds to do as I rush to the car in the morning.

I don't attend *taalim* and can't recite the six points, but I have a great love for reading *seerah* and *tafseer*, and take pleasure in learning about our great faith where I can.

I haven't done Banting, Atkins or Weight Watchers diets; my favourite foods are mutton *biryani*, *dhal* and rice, and, of course, an 'Akhals'* toasted French polony special, so I've made my peace with those few extra kilos I carry.

So no, I'm not the go-to person for nuggets of wisdom about living a perfect life, but what I can share are my humble lessons of a life well lived, and what I have learnt from having loved and lost (and loved again).

I have loved. I know I am capable of deep emotion for another, for selfless giving, for the meeting of minds and hearts. I learnt that love does not possess and it does not diminish you. I know for sure that there isn't one soulmate or one love of your life. Sometimes things don't work out. There is no shame in divorce, when you had sincere intentions and tried your best to make it work. "Perhaps you love a thing and it is bad for you" (*Surah* 2, Verse 216).

I have lost and have recovered from it. I rebounded stronger, more capable of giving and receiving love, knowing better what I wanted and needed in a partner. I learnt for sure that losing a guy is not the end of your life and often, when one door closes another door opens to better things. "Surely with every difficulty there is relief" (*Surah* 94, Verse 6).

Know thyself. Through difficult times, I have tested my mettle, uncovered strength, endurance, resilience and a capacity to pick myself up and begin another day. I learnt to look critically at what determined my self-worth. Strip the titles you give yourself, like wife, mother, daughter, professional, *Muslimah* and ask: What qualities serve you? What presence do you hold in the lives of others? What contribution is uniquely yours? What legacy will you leave? How will your time on this earth be remembered?

Have a tribe to belong to. I truly believe that what has carried me through difficult times are the meaningful connections that I have developed. Every woman needs her crowd of supporters – faithful family and fierce friendships. My 'sisterhood' has served as solace at times and back-up when called for. I have experienced the restorative and healing power in a circle of true female friends. I don't mean superficial acquaintances. The deep bonds I talk of are free of jealousy, competition and judgement.

Give and receive. There is wisdom to be found everywhere and an abundance of people who can serve as your role models. I have been fortunate to find unique spirits who have been my coaches, mentors and guides, some in my professional life and others in my personal life. I have benefited from their experience, life lessons and wisdom. In turn, I realise that I have the capacity to give back in the same powerful way to others.

Develop style and grace. My biggest kindness to myself is that I don't look for perfection or the perception of perfection in everything that I do. The blushing bride, the immaculate homemaker, the domestic queen, the fashionable *hijabista*, the achieving academic, the highflying career woman; it must be exhausting to try to keep up that image all the time. So, I've learnt to just be me. I seek not to create a life that is the envy of everyone. It's okay to just be okay. It really is enough. To be God-conscious, to have a home where Allah's name is remembered, to raise wholesome kids, to keep a job that pays the bills and stimulates the mind, to put a nourishing plate of food on the table...that's winning in this game of life! I am abundantly grateful, all the time, and remind myself just how blessed I am. As Cat Stevens (Yusuf Islam) sang, "Take your time, think a lot, think of everything you got".

Support girl power! Raise daughters AND SONS who are feminists – please. And I don't mean angry Western women fighting for sexual permissiveness. Islamic feminism takes its roots from the Quranic prescripts of equality for all human beings, in worship and in everyday life. Within the safe, protective bounds of our religious code, there is space for woman to own an equal place in the world. Many women who have come before me have been victim to stereotyping, narrow-mindedness and uninformed conventions.

We don't have to perpetuate the cycle of repression played out for generations, where women themselves stood in judgement and participated in limiting their daughters' and sisters' potentials. Now, as mothers, we stand at a threshold, with the power to cause seismic shifts and transform the paths of our children. Our daughters should believe in their capacity to think and do and contribute in the world; and our sons should believe that their mothers, sisters, wives and daughters are not subhuman because of their lack of a Y chromosome.

Growing up, I was surrounded by strong, open-minded aunts and girl cousins, who dealt with adversity, including divorce, financial struggle and loss of loved ones, with great tenacity, kindness and also humour. I was surrounded by gentle uncles and male cousins, who helped to cook, tend to their children or continued to write love letters to their wives into their old age. I was never told "girls can't do that" or "we don't do such things" (except once, when I braided my hair; and my grandfather was right, it was a particularly bad idea). I received only support and encouragement in everything I pursued. Everyone around me celebrated my successes, shared in my achievements and believed in my dreams and ambitions. I've never known naysayers. I've learnt that overcoming challenges is often a matter of mind-set, not principle. The world can change if we are prepared to think of things in a different way.

I have thought a lot about my marriage and divorce and this is what I have to offer. Choose your partner well. And then, when you have chosen, love your partner well. Be mates who recognise and celebrate each other's strengths and abilities. Be partners who stand side by side and acknowledge that, despite your differences, you have equal value and make equal contributions. Seek not the love of Mills and Boons or Bollywood movies. Let the noble example of our beloved Prophet (PBUH) and his cherished wife *Hadrat* Khadijah serve as a model for a marriage founded on mutual respect, deep admiration, unwavering commitment and profound trust in each other. "Her love had been nurtured in my heart by Allah Himself" (Sahih Muslim Book 31: 5972). We should hope to provide love that nourishes our partner and receive the same from him.

On that note, let me end my story, although it's not really an ending but rather an exciting new chapter. You see, I have found love again and I am embarking on a new leg of my journey, with happy days ahead, *Insha'Allah*. He is a good man, softly spoken and humble, a man of his word, with good character, strong *imaan* and so steadfast in *sabr*. I am older, wiser and hopefully better equipped for making a marriage work. I embrace the fact that I am human and oh, so flawed, but with a kind heart, fierce mind and brave spirit, I intend to live simply and make a peaceful, happy home.

Let the last words be those of American writer Bessie Anderson Stanley: "She has achieved success who has lived well, laughed often and loved much".

---

* Akhals is short for Akhalwayas, which is a name of a popular take-away food business in South Africa.

55

Feeling beautiful in a marriage

Hawa Bibi Shahaboodien

It is almost 12h30 on a Monday afternoon. When my last client of the morning leaves, I rush off to fetch my son from preschool. I hurriedly leave the preschool parking to pick up my daughter from her school. She's in grade one, and like every mother sharing this new experience, I am anxious about different routines and life changes.

Once we get home, we eat lunch and then cram in some school homework, before I take the children to *madressah*. I work until 5 pm, collect the children from *madressah*, and assist them with their homework. While they work, I cook. My husband returns from work and we eat supper together as a family. He then spends leisure time with the children and before 8 pm, we put them to bed. We then spend some alone time together before retiring for the day.

Today is just another day like countless others, where I do a juggling act between my many different roles – mother, career woman, housekeeper and wife. I own a hair, laser and beauty salon and I work almost seven days a week, as I do hair and make up for brides and weddings on weekends. In 2016, I worked as the hairdresser and make-up artist for the Miss India SA pageant. I have also been featured in many newspapers. Balancing work and the rest of my life is challenging, but I ensure that my family's needs always come first.

I think back to my single days when I had big aspirations and dreams to become somebody, but everybody else saw marriage as being of ultimate importance. From the tender age of seventeen, *samoosa* run candidates stalked me, but I am a strong believer in *taqdeer*. I believe that I will only get that which is meant for me.

After experiencing far too many *samoosa* runs, I became physically and mentally exhausted. I begged my parents to give me space to pursue my dreams. My parents agreed and I finally got a chance to focus on my studies, which I enjoyed tremendously.

I became an internationally qualified sophrologist, and an internationally qualified hairdresser. I also earned an international diploma in teaching. I then became an aerobics instructor. I finally pursued a diploma in interior design.

And then, at the age of 23 I married and happily mastered the skill of being a wife and career woman. My daughter, Tahseen was born soon after. My life was perfect.

However, life is never without tragedy. When pregnant with my son, my eldest brother had a car accident and tragically passed away. "Surely we belong to Allah and to him we shall return" (*Surah* 2, Verse 156).

My brother's sudden death rocked our lives but I kept a brave face. As women, we are pillars of strength for our families. We spend most of our time looking after everyone else and often forget to care for ourselves. As the airplane safety video tells passengers, "Put on your own oxygen mask first"...you cannot take care of others if you're running out of air yourself. Like every other human being, I have a special light inside of me, and every time I neglect myself, that light dims.

I have learnt to love myself and I know how to highlight my beauty, allowing it to shine through to others. I know that when I dress well and improve my appearance, people begin to pay more attention to me; they listen to me, seek my company and ask for my opinions. When we dress well and take care of our hair and skin and apply a little makeup, it affects the behaviour of those around us in a positive way. And that makes us feel better and increases our confidence and self-esteem.

Even in my crazy, demanding life, I take time to care for myself, because only then will I have more energy and love to share with others around me. I know that my confidence enhances my beauty. When I feel good about myself, I give off a positive aura, which attracts others to me. I don't have the time to take luxurious holidays but I often treat myself in small ways. Small changes can make a big difference. A facial every now and then, a little make up or just a relaxing massage makes me feel good and look good.

A facial improves the skin's tone, texture and elasticity by counteracting the damaging effects of air pollution and sun exposure. Facial exfoliation helps to remove dead skin cells and free radicals, which cause premature aging; it also removes black heads and improves the appearance of the skin. Your skin feels refreshed and relaxed. The facial massage alone works wonders on tired, dehydrated and wrinkled skin. It also encourages lymphatic drainage as it flushes out toxins, while promoting circulation. The best part about getting a facial is that the results are instant. Rarely do you find a product that lives up to your expectations. After just one facial you will see an immediate improvement in the appearance of your skin and your skin will continue to feel good for the next three to four weeks.

I often wonder why women look their best before marriage and then, when married, they offer excuses of having "no time". I am not being selfish for taking care of myself first, because I know that everybody around me deserves a happy, positive Hawa Bibi. I am no superwoman. I am a woman.

"If you want to be original, be ready to be copied" (Coco Chanel)

Jamela Garda

Whoohaa! And they lived happily...ever...after. Yeah, right. There is no such thing. But of course, as a follower of the Islamic faith, I know that nothing on this earth is forever. And therefore I will always live life to the fullest!

I and my husband of 33 years are very blessed. The wedding ring did not come with a manual but we tweaked life as we went along and made it all happen. Of course, we added just the right dosage of respect, style, grace and dignity. Gosh! Imagine if every person and every marriage were the same, how boring would this place called earth, be? Fortunately we are our own kind of crazy and that makes life so interesting and colourful.

Ashraf and I look for the small things that complement each other, even if they are on the opposite sides of the spectrum. This task is hard work and immensely challenging at times, but my best advice to all couples is to communicate, communicate, communicate. Always give your support, love and loyalty. I believe that only if you truly want to make your marriage work, will you find the common road. Be efficient but be spontaneous. And don't forget the sense of humour. A good laugh lifts the spirits. Eat, pray and travel together.

We have date nights. We share common interests in certain things. We go to sporting events together; we love watching a great game of cricket. We enjoy dinner with friends. We play board games. We hold hands when shopping. We enjoy our grandson and the love and joy that he brings into our lives. Because of work commitments and time constraints, we only manage to pray two *salaahs* together on any given day, but we make this time special. Our small secret is that…before we begin the prayer, we lock our pinky fingers together and remind ourselves that we still love each other. This ritual is a special moment we share and I look forward to it every day. Ssshhhh…It is our secret, after all.

People often ask me if I am always so happy and vibrant and full of life and I reply, "Yes, I try." I do have my moods, trust me, my family will vouch for that. I believe that it is important to treat people well, with a kind, generous nature that leaves a lasting impression. At the same time, however, it is important that you are happy, too. It must not be a case of 'Oooops, the mask fell off!' Living life involves balancing your act and you will feel satisfied within the depths of your heart when you do it well.

For me, style is not a fashion item. Style is what you wear on your face and in your heart; it is the most sincere smile and the most generous, kind and caring heart. Style is the outer manifestation of your inner soul. You project style. No money can buy it. I often think of a French clown or busker with his white jumpsuit with big black buttons down the centre, pointy hat and black tassel, and his white painted face and a bright red smile. He is pretty stylish. Style is not about how much money you spent on your outfit or how expensive your suit is or the jewellery you wear. Style is the full package. It is how you carry yourself, how you interact with others and make them feel.

You have to love yourself first to ooze the confidence that style requires. If you respect and love yourself as much as you should, it becomes pretty clear how to find your own style. You will know which clothes suit you and complement your lifestyle, and, most importantly, your body. You should be comfortable. You should be elegant.

It is important to welcome only positive thoughts and positive people in your space, to allow the best of you to shine. Your mind is a powerful thing. When you fill it with powerful thoughts, your life will change.

You have to add value to the room you enter into. You have to leave that same room leaving a lasting impression. You have to be confident and fearless. You should never care what other people say or think about you. You have to own your space and make it your own kind of crazy. Your unique style. That special way that makes you...YOU.

My late mother was one of the kindest, most elegant, stylish women I know. She made everybody feel so special and everyone loved being around her. She always had a good word for everyone and the most beautiful smile. She was my Audrey Hepburn look alike. I often take a leaf out of her book. She always offered great advice. One particular piece comes to mind – we were doing Eid shopping and mother said to me, "Don't forget to buy yourself a new nightgown. It is Eid, after all." Oi, yoi, yoi! We had a good laugh but it made complete sense. Mother was spot on.

Style means looking good and feeling good all the time. It's a 24/7 kind of feeling, even when you sleep: no tracksuits, no old fashioned nighties. No, no, no. And a big YES, to your underwear being pretty. You know how good you feel when you like what you are wearing under your clothes. That brings confidence.

I learnt a lot from my mother, and Coco Chanel, too. I love this Coco line: "If you want to be original, be ready to be copied." I created my own style and I interpret it in the way I understand it and am comfortable with. I live with passion and style that is uniquely me.

Never be sorry for who you are. Your personality should never be shrouded in what society expects of you. Be shamelessly, unapologetically, YOU. Be unique, the creator of your own style. But keep it real. My last piece of advice, a phrase I coined myself: don't let the honeymoon end.

Pearls of wisdom

• •

You are enough. Believe that. **Razina Theba**

Don't lose yourself – pursue your interests and be a whole person, without needing anyone to complete you.
Aneesa Bodiat-Sujee

As women, we are given the highest status in the home and with our children. Embrace this confidently and trust yourself and your instincts. Respect is earned by respecting yourself and others. **Raashida Khan**

Self-love is more important than people pleasing. (You cannot feed your family if your cup is empty.) **Afzad-Al**

Don't allow cooking, the in-laws or any other petty matters turn you into a resentful, manipulative and angry person. Embrace your marriage positively and fill it with all things beautiful; thoughts, ideas and moments. Financial standing is not the deciding factor of the success of a marriage, and don't allow it to be. **Somayya Hansrod**

Don't feel you're not good enough. Do your best according to the teachings of Muhammed (PBUH) and the Quran and know that that is the best. Be a proud Muslimah wife.
Maymoonah Chohan

Give to yourself first, so that you become a powerful woman in your own right. What we give to ourselves in love, respect, acceptance, etc. creates the confident, strong, sexy, loving beings that we project into the world. **Khalida Moosa**

Marriage will not complete you. Find yourself first. Love yourself first. Always remember that there's a life beyond marriage, and I'm not referring to work or leisure. I refer to your Islamic obligation to contribute positively to the lives of others. **Zaheera Jina**

About the authors

Afzad-Al is a registered holistic counsellor, play and trauma therapist. She works from home when she's not plagued by the challenges of chronic fatigue caused by CMT (a hereditary neuropathy, a type of muscular dystrophy). However, she doesn't let it get her down. Instead, she uses her situation to her advantage, enjoying her hobbies of reading and more reading, and living vicariously through others.

Layla Abdullah-Poulos is an award-winning writer with an extensive background in literary criticism. She has a Bachelor's degree in Historical Studies and Literature, a Master's in Liberal Studies, and an Advanced Certificate in Women's and Gender Studies. Layla presently teaches history, as an adjunct instructor, and novel writing skills, as a coach. In 2017, Layla received the Francis Award from The International Association for the Study of Popular Romance (IASPR). Her peer-reviewed journal article, "The Stable Muslim Love Triangle – Triangular Desire in Black Muslim Romance Fiction" will be published in the Journal of Popular Romance Studies in 2018. She just completed her first romance novel, My Way to You. In 2017, she accepted a position as acquisitions editor for Djarabi Kitabs Publishing, a Muslim publishing house seeking to amplify diverse voices. Layla is also managing editor for the NbA Muslims blog on the Patheos Muslim Channel. The blog highlights the heritages, experiences, and cultural productions of native-born American Muslims of African American, indigenous, Latinx, and European descent. She frequently writes book reviews for NbA Muslims, as well as conducts online interviews with Muslim authors for NbA Muslim Authors Speak. Layla enjoys a reputation for giving insightful and critically-constructive literary reviews.

Shakira Akabor has taught in a mainstream classroom since 2003. In 2012 she left the teaching profession to further her studies. She is currently a PhD candidate in Inclusive Education at the University of the Witwatersrand (Wits). Shakira's research interests are on pedagogies for diverse learners and the ways in which we can include rather than exclude learners in the classroom. At present, she works as an independent contractor at both Wits and University of South Africa (UNISA). Shakira lives with her husband and three children in Centurion, Gauteng.

Najma Ansari is writer, speaker and community activist. She has a degree in Business and a Master's in International Relations. She has worked in the print media/journalism, which has given her unique insights into social behaviour across cultures. She has been fortunate to have had international exposure, having lived in Asia, Europe, America and Africa and is comfortable with many languages. She values assisting community engagements by facilitating workshops and classes. She enjoys creative work and writes poetry in her free time. Her blog is https://najmanotebook.wordpress.com.

Feroza Arbee was raised in rural Mpumalanga with a strong sense of community and social responsibility. After completing her schooling, she moved to Johannesburg, where she obtained her undergraduate medical degree. She met her husband and married while still a student. She had her firstborn while specialising as a psychiatrist. Currently, she is a married mother of three and runs a limited psychiatric practice. After observing the challenges faced by her mother and other women in her family, as well as her own experiences, Feroza has developed a keen interest in women's coping skills and mental health. She is fascinated by cultural and religious influences on the presentation of mental illness, treatment preferences and social perceptions. She strongly advocates social awareness and de-stigmatisation of mental illness, especially in the Indian Muslim community.

Saaleha Idrees Bamjee is a photographer and writer based in Johannesburg. She has a Master's degree in Creative Writing and is the winner of the 2014 Writivism Short Story Prize. Her poetry has appeared in *New Contrast, New Coin, Ons Klyntji, Aerodrome* and the *Sol Plaatje European Union Poetry* anthologies, among others, as well as the special South African issue of *Illuminations* magazine by the University of Charleston, South Carolina, USA. Her work has also been included in Van Schaik Publishers' *Voices of this Land: An Anthology of South African Poetry in English*. She was the Writivism Emerging African Writers resident at Stellenbosch University in October 2016. Her debut collection of poetry is forthcoming from uHlanga Press in 2018. Access her work online at www.saaleha.com and www.shootcake.com or follow her on twitter.com/saaleha and instagram.com/saaleha_b.

Fatima Bheekoo-Shah lives in Gauteng and is a published writer for various magazines. She is also the author for the popular food series, Musings of a Foodie, currently being compiled into a book. A book nerd and avid reader, she is always looking for her next great read.

Aneesa Bodiat-Sujee is a *Muslimah*, in love with pencils, books and flat shoes. She is sometimes a lawyer, but mostly a writer and editor, always in search of the perfect sentence.

Adela Bootha practises independently as a psychometrist, and has over twenty years' experience in psychological assessments and organisational development. She also has more than five years' experience as a counsellor. She has a wide-ranging work experience, including in the banking and retail sectors, and has travelled extensively within South Africa and beyond to conduct psychological assessments for team building, career counselling, relationship building and staff development for Vodacom. Apart from her practice, Adela serves as an associate for Mediate Works and for The Talent Hub and she is a volunteer at a family counselling centre. To connect with Adela: www.mediateworks.co.za.

Saffiya Ismail Cassim was born in Pietermaritzburg and she now resides in Johannesburg. Her biggest accomplishment in life is being a mother; everything else pales in comparison. Saffiya is a contributing author to *Riding the Samoosa Express: Personal Narratives of Marriage and Beyond* by Zaheera Jina and Hasina Asvat. Saffiya's past credits include editing *Islam – A Religion of Peace* by Saleem Ahmed. She is a regular columnist for *Indian Spice*, and has contributed articles to *Women24*, *News24*, *Ladysmith Gazette*, *Al-Qalam* and *Huffington Post*. She was nominated in *Cosmopolitan* magazine for Mover and Shaker of the Year Award and also received a 100% Human Award from East Coast Radio. Saffiya has survived many challenges since her last chapter in *Riding the Samoosa Express*. She says, "This is the new me, I simply put back the pieces differently. I make every moment count because I am not promised the next."

Maymoona Rajah Chohan is a dedicated mum, wife, grandmother, sister, daughter and friend. She is a radiographer by profession, and has added to her many skills by completing courses with Lifeline, Johannesburg Association for the aged (JAFTA), and in cardiac rehabilitation. Maymoona has recently resigned from her fulltime work to go back to her main passion: doing charity work and assisting whenever and wherever she can. She is also a volunteer at the Cancer Association of South Africa (CANSA) Westrand. Although outspoken at times, Maymoona prefers to work silently in the background. She has two adult daughters and one son. Originally form Marlboro, Maymoona now lives in Azaadville with her husband and son.

Sabera Chothia teaches Muslim women the practices of Islam. She sits on the board of the adult care center in Lenasia and also belongs to Disabled Information Support Group (DISA). She assists poor families who are in need of groceries and basic necessities. Sabera lives in Lenasia with her son, daughter-in-law and two beautiful granddaughters.

Khairun-Nisaa Dadipatel is a young widowed mother of two children, Abu Bakr and Zinneerah. She teaches in the day. She is also an artist who loves painting. Her paintings are on exhibit at the Grayston Gallery in Wynberg, Sandton.

Quraisha Dawood is a mom, wife, academic, baker and mosaic maker. She received her PhD in Sociology in 2016 and is the director of Write on Q, which assists students with writing and editing their dissertations. Her research has been published in academic journals and regional newspapers, while her creative work has been published in anthologies such as *Belly of Fire* and the *Readers Digest*. She writes a monthly column for *Al-Ummah*. In her spare time, she loves experimenting in the kitchen, reading and watching Thomas and Friends with her son.

Mariam B. Daya is a reader, writer, adventurer, child counsellor, blogger, and student of life...

Yasmin Denat holds a Bachelor of Arts with Honours in Publishing and Editing. The written word has always been her intense passion and her dreams of being a writer have never quite diminished. Yasmin lives in Azaadville and is the mother to four kindred souls.

Ayesha Desai, from Pretoria, has enjoyed reading and imagining stories all her life. She has been writing stories since she was a teenager, but *Jasmine in the Wind* is the first book she has published. Ayesha enjoys plotting twists and turns for her latest work, writing poetry and flash fiction stories for a culturally diverse readership, and posting rather long Facebook rants about modern parenting methods. When she isn't working on her writing, you can find her baking, painting, and enjoying the outdoors with her husband and two children. Ayesha also works in the corporate world as a training facilitator, runs her own company, which specialises in teen empowerment, and is a motivational speaker.

Papatia Feauxzar is an American author and publisher of West African descent who lives in Dallas, Texas with her son and husband. She holds a master's degree in accounting. After working as an accountant for a corporate firm for almost five years, Papatia decided to pursue a career from home, while home-schooling her son. In May 2013, she founded Djarabi Kitabs Publishing and in April 2017 she opened Fofky's, an Online Book and Coffee/Tea Shop. Papatia sells a range of things, including Muslim cosmetics, jewellery and stationary. Besides being a trader of Muslim and Islamicate merchandise,

Papatia has written for many online platforms, such as *Hayati*, *Khadijahi*, and *SISTERS* magazines, MVSLIM, and AboutIslam. You can learn more at www.djarabikitabs.com.

Gouwa Gabier was born and raised in Johannesburg, and is the youngest of three daughters. She was born in the 80's, schooled in the 90's, and married in the naughties (2006). Gouwa worked in corporate, founded a successful business, and then owned a franchise. She is now a mother to three energetic, adventurous, affectionate children. Gouwa competently juggles her various professions: a taxi driver who races to multiple pick-up times; a nutritionist who plans healthy lunchboxes for her family; a play date participant; and organiser of and regular guest at children's birthday parties. She strives to make sure all the boxes are ticked, while searching for the famous 'me time'. She is supported and loved by her husband.

Jamela Garda has an infectious personality that radiates her zest for the good things in life. Her quest to enjoy life in the moment impacts on all whom she meets. A stylish mother of four and doting grandmother of one, she likes to remind everyone that she is 21 and will be 21 forever. She loves food (especially Turkish food) and travel – especially to Turkey. Jamela is strong-willed, fiercely loyal, very driven, strongly believes Allah guides her through everything, and is very grateful for being so blessed. She is a relentless social media user and believes that a selfie or two is a great way to commemorate a great day. During her Hajj Pilgrimage to Makah in 1438/2017, Jamela inspired many South Africans by her unique personal insights on social media. #SayALilPrayerForMe is one of her many catchphrases and she never fails to shout, "Whoohaa!" when surrounded by friends.

Newlyweds draw inspiration from her whispered advice, "Never let the honeymoon end!" Follow her on Instagram.

Maimoonah Gori is a qualified author, teacher and business woman who runs creative writing courses for young minds and special needs kids. With a decade in the literacy field, she has a passion for teaching and the world of words. She is a self-published author, and has published 12 children's Islamic books and a novella. A creative at heart, Maimoonah's Nur ul Kidz brand has created a range of niche products for Muslim gifting, such as cards, magnets and notebooks. Nur ul Kidz also publishes an annual anthology of stories and standalone books produced by young authors.

Rehana Gunduwalla (Moosajee), also known as "The Barefoot Facilitator" is committed to bridging divides and building connections. Drawing on her former experiences as educator, community activist and local government councillor in the City of Johannesburg, Rehana creates opportunities that encourage people to bridge social and spiritual divides. She also weaves her rich and sometimes painful life experiences into the sessions, to create authentic conversation. She is the mother to two young adults, Aadil and Faheemah.

Somayya Hansrod is married and has four kids. Her passion for teaching has led her to pursue her lifelong dream of operating a home-schooling facilitation centre. While her road to the kitchen is still a very bumpy one, with many a detour, Somayya is an avid reader, and being a member of the Roshnee book club for the past 12 years has fuelled her love for the written word. Writing, she feels, is therapy for her soul, and she aspires to write a storybook for children.

Waasila Jassat is a single mum of a thirteen-year-old boy. She is a medical doctor and is currently doing her PhD, specialising in public health. Waasila's faith and family have instilled in her the need to serve others and to pursue social justice for disadvantaged and marginalised people. She has been helping to start a leadership programme for activists working to address the causes of poor health. She loves travel, good food and huge get-togethers with family and friends.

Zaheera Jina holds a PhD in Mathematics Education from the University of the Witwatersrand in South Africa. She is also a co-editor and contributing author of the anthology, *Riding the Samoosa Express: Personal Narratives of Marriage and Beyond*. Zaheera is the founder of Jozi's Books and Blogs Festivities (Jozisbbf), a non-profit organisation that aims to cultivate a culture of reading and writing in South Africa through various literary events. *Surprise!* is her first children's book and is published by Djarabi Kitabs Publishing in Texas, USA. She lives in Lenasia with her husband, three sons and many in-laws.

Safeera Kaka is a journalist and radio presenter who resides in Johannesburg. She studied journalism at Rhodes University. She hosts a popular magazine programme on Cii Radio, four times a week. Her show has a large global audience and tackles various issues, including mental health awareness, social development and upliftment, analysis of contemporary society and spiritual development. The show also focuses heavily on the empowerment of women. Safeera also hosts media development workshops in Johannesburg to get young people interested in Islamic radio and media. She takes a keen interest in humanitarian matters, and on her recent return from Turkey gave a first-hand account on the challenges faced by Syrian Refugees after the civil war. She serves as a member of the NGO, Cii Projects, and has helped to spearhead a nationwide campaign to clothe children in conflict zones for

Eid. She also takes a keen interest in all things culinary and regularly shares her kitchen adventures on social media.

Fatima Kazee is an admitted attorney with an LLB degree from the University of Johannesburg. She currently works for the Jozikids Directory as a website administrator. She writes articles on parenting for the zaparents blog and is also a contributor to *The Huffington Post South Africa*. Fatima cooks only so that her family will survive and prefers to spend her time reading and researching. She lives in Johannesburg with her husband, two sons and a little princess with a magical unicorn.

Raashida Khan is a content creator, author, poet, wife, mother and friend. As a caring, compassionate and empathetic person who loves observing people and life, she is a storyteller of note. She would like to be remembered as 'never boring.' She is 49 and was born in Durban (her favourite city), where she lived for 27 years before moving to Johannesburg. She qualified with a BA Hons (Economic History) from the University of Kwa-Zulu Natal. Her short story, 'Your Voice, My Strength' was selected as the winning entry for the 2017 South African Muslim Women's Short Story Competition and was published in *Irtiqa Online*. Another short story, 'It's not Funny', appears in *Happy Holidays: Anthology of Short Stories*, available on Amazon. She plans to self-publish an anthology of poetry and three novels, in 2018. In the meanwhile, she continues penning poems and the occasional social commentary blog. Read her writings and musings at www.raashisreflections.com.

Sumayya Mehtar (aka 'Desert Moon') is the director of Medix pharmacy in Florida, South Africa. She returned to South Africa four years ago, after spending almost five years in the

Najd region of Saudi Arabia, working as an emergency pharmacist. Her work as a pharmacist at world class hospitals has enabled her to meet and treat famous individuals, including Nelson Mandela, African presidents, television personalities, and royal family members based in the Middle East region. She is also the presenter of the weekly Arab news segment on Radio Al Ansaar. She won the prestigious 'Woman of Wonder' award in 2017 for being a voice to the voiceless, in addition to creating a positive impact within her community. She has also contributed to the book *Riding the Samoosa Express: Personal Narratives of Marriage and Beyond*. All proceeds from her blog, *Desert Moon's Diary* are given away to charity.

Shauqeen Mizaj is a journalist working for a leading Malayalam daily in Kerala, India. She writes for *CHIPS*, the weekly English supplement of the daily's Gulf edition. Born in 1983, she graduated in Engineering from the University of Calicut in 2006 and also received a Diploma in Web Designing and Animation in 2013. After a brief stint at teaching and two years working at Interactive, an online portal, she ended up in the field of journalism and writing, a partial fulfilment of her dream of becoming a writer. Shauqeen is currently pursuing a Diploma in Journalism and Mass Communication. A bookworm who loves the smell of books; she also adores the tantalising aromas of early morning coffee and her mom's fish curry, and the fresh, earthy fragrance after the first rain. She resides in Calicut, Kerala with her husband and two kids. When she isn't glued to her monitor, she spends time reading, painting pottery, doing craftwork and running after her two kids. She is currently working on a book on various flavours of the Malabar region in Kerala. You can reach her at shauqimizaj@gmail.com.

N. Moola is an educator, motivational speaker and writer who believes that words have the power to turn dreams into reality. Passionate about education and uplifting humanity, she is an advocate for instilling the gift of reading into the lives of children and adults alike. N. Moola hopes to enrich communities through the written and spoken word, by motivating and uplifting the youth through reading and creative self-expression. Living as a single mum, N. Moola favours the underdog and believes that challenges can be overcome through immense strength and inner motivation: "Without belief we cannot achieve."

Khalida Moosa is interested in narratives that defy social norms. She is attracted to writing that breaks boundaries and addresses gender inequality and sexual and cultural stereotypes. Her poems have appeared in *The #Coinage Book One* and *Type/Cast*. She has previously hosted a community book club and enjoys liaising with writers and artists who open debate and discussion. She is a passionate bookaholic who believes books can change the world.

Zayboon Motala is a teacher by profession. She is the author of a craft book and also a contributing author to *Riding the Samoosa Express: Personal Narratives of Marriage and Beyond*. Zayboon is involved in social work in South Africa and its neighbouring countries. She met with a bad accident and only walked again after eleven years of disability. She has a school named in her honour.

Hina Nafe was born and brought up in Pakistan. She is presently a practising chartered accountant at one of the top four firms in New Zealand. Besides accounting and numbers, Hina enjoys writing. Follow her on: http://www.hinasworld.com/.

Nurnazida Nazri is currently a legal practitioner and used to teach law at a public university for more than ten years. She has authored three books: *Submitting to Allah*, *Candle in the Wind* and *Law of Contract Made Simple for Laymen*, which are available on Amazon, Payhip and E-Sentral. Teaching and writing have always been her passion and she would hate to miss them even for one day. She can be contacted at ziedanazri@gmail.com.

Nabeela Noorani was born and raised in a multicultural family in Port Elizabeth. She was educated in Port Elizabeth, where she went on to teach at high school level. She also lived and taught briefly in Mombasa, Kenya. After self-publishing her novel, Six Broken Hearts, she embarked on a dream of opening up her own independent publishing house, TOSH Publishing, which has seen four published books since its inception in September 2017. She lives in South Africa again and is married with three children.

Dilshad Parker is a graphic designer and blogger by day and supermom and master chef by night; or so she would like to believe. Her foodie obsession has her always on the prowl for the latest places to feature on her website, www.hungryforhalaal.co.za. You'll usually find her at a restaurant, ahem, doing photoshoots of her food...

Nabihah Plaatjes is an award-winning entrepreneur and change agent, who, as one of the founding members of iloveza.com, 'plays her part' in the development and empowerment of others. Her passions include writing and marketing, and she holds a Bachelor of Arts degree, with majors in Culture, Communication, Media Studies, and English.

Shaakira Rahiman Saleh is the co-director of the marketing company, Lilac Design Studio. She also serves as assistant editor of Roshgold News. She is the zealous mother of three: Asma, Nusaybah and Muhammad Bilal. She is grateful to be married to her best friend, Zuber Saleh.

Mumtaz Moosa Saley is a lifestyle blogger, published author and mother to four amazing, busy kids. Mumtaz currently resides in Johannesburg and hopes to make a difference through her blogs.

Yumna Samaria was born, raised and educated in Pretoria, and married in Roshnee. She holds a summa cum laude Bachelor of Education Degree from the University of the Witwatersrand, where she graduated with a melting pot of majors, including Psychology, Music, English and the Arts. Yumna has also studied to be part of the international La Leche League and The Cancer Awareness Association, and is currently completing an Islamic Careline Counselling Course. Yumna taught at primary and secondary school levels. While she does not enjoy aerobics or strenuous exercise, she revels in baking exquisite brownies and cream-smothered goodies. She runs a home-based business and is also a member of the Vaal Muslim Women's Forum and Roshnee book club. Yumna resides in Roshnee with her husband and daughter.

Hawa Bibi Shahaboodien holds international diplomas in hairdressing and beauty therapy. She is also a qualified aerobics instructor. In 2016, Hawa Bibi was a make-up artist for the Miss India SA pageant. She has also been featured in the *Lenasia Times*, *Benoni City Times*, *Heidelburg Heraut* and the *Balfour Herald*. Hawa Bibi owns her own laser, hair and beauty salon in Lakefield, Benoni, where she lives with her husband, two daughters and son.

Safiyyah Sujee is a qualified chartered accountant. She studied accounting sciences at the University of Pretoria and completed her honours degree through UNISA, as one of the top 50 best performing students in the country. At 25 years of age, Safiyyah was recently honoured with a national Women of Wonder award for inspiring and making a difference in society. She has her own monthly column in the *Laudium Sun* and writes for the *Lenasia Times* on an ad-hoc basis. She partakes in regular interactive discussions on Radio Islam, aimed at opening people's minds to new ideas, spreading kindness and stimulating interest in particular topics – with a hint of humour. From time to time, she also does motivational and other forms of public speaking, but is most well known for her blogs and videos on Facebook and Instagram (@safhappens). Behind the light-hearted humour and short video clips, good for a laugh after a hard day, Saffiyah hides some valuable life lessons.

Safiyyah Surtee is a graduate of Arabic and Islamic Studies, currently completing her Master's degree in the Study of Islam, with a focus on gender. She is an avid writer, dabbling in freelance journalism, and a community activist, concerned mainly with Muslim women's issues – Safiyaah advocates for the participation of Muslim women at all levels of religious life. She has worked at the Afro-Middle East Centre previously, and is a contributor to *Muslimah Media Watch*, where she critiques representations of Muslim women in the media. Safiyyah is also a teaching fellow in the Study of Islam at the University of Johannesburg. She is the co-founder of Faithworks, a network of South African Muslim women, running activities like *halaqat* retreats, interfaith and solidarity events, film screenings and more. Safiyyah is a committee member of Masjid ul-Islam, where she serves the congregation. She lives in Johannesburg with her husband, Ebrahim, and their twin girls.

Razina Theba holds Bachelor of Arts and Bachelor of Law degrees from the University of Witwatersrand. She is an attorney and lectures labour law on a part-time basis for the Department of Industrial Psychology at the University of Johannesburg. She shares her home in Johannesburg with her husband, two teenage sons and an adored cat.

Zara Valli is the author of the fiction novel, *Kryolia: The Quest for the Medallion*. She wrote the novel inspired by her love for fantasy and the stories her mother used to narrate to her as a child. She has always had a passion for writing and is working on children's books and a compilation of poems. Zara is a high school educator, and is completing her Honours in Education Management. Find out more about Zara on Facebook (zaravalli) and Instagram (@zaravalli).

Glossary

aalim – (Arabic) male scholar

aalima – (Arabic) female scholar

aalo – potato

Aameen – (Aramaic) So be it

aamil – (Arabic) spiritual doctor

aamli – (Gujerati) tamarind

achaar – (Persian) a type of pickle in which the food is preserved in spiced oil

adhan – (Arabic) Islamic call to prayer

akhlaq – (Arabic) practice of virtue, morality and manners

akhni – (Urdu) broth with rice, meat and vegetables

Alhamdulillah – (Arabic) All praise be to Allah

ameer – (Arabic) leader

apakhala – (Gujerati) mother's oldest sister

awliya – (Arabic) supporter, guardian, protector

baji – (Hindi) older sister

barakah – (Arabic) blessings

biryani – (Persian) rice dish made from spices, rice, mutton, chicken, fish or vegetables

Bismillah – (Arabic) In the name of Allah and upon the blessings of Allah

burfee – (Hindi) a dense milk-based sweet confectionery (mithai) from the Indian subcontinent; originally from India, the name is a derivative of 'barf' (snow)

burqah – (Arabic) a long, loose garment covering the hair of a woman

chapati – (Hindi) a form of roti or rotta (bread)

chevro – (Gujerati) snack with peanuts and cornflakes

chotifooi – (Gujerati) father's youngest sister

chotikhala – (Gujerati) mother's youngest sister

daadi – (Gujerati) paternal grandmother

dhania – (Hindi) corriander

dheg – (Gujerati) large pot of food

dhikr – (Arabic) reciting the praises of Allah and his beloved Prophet Muhammad (PBUH)

dhuhr – (Arabic) noon prayer

duah – (Arabic) act of supplication

Eid – Islamic celebration

Eid-ul-Adha – (Arabic) the Muslim festival marking the end of the annual pilgrimage to Mecca and commemorating the sacrifice of Ebrahim

esha – (Arabic) Islamic night prayer

faskh – (Arabic) a divorce granted by a judge

fatwah – (Arabic) a legal opinion or ruling issued by an Islamic scholar

fiqh – (Arabic) Islamic law. Deep understanding or full comprehension

fooi – (Gujerati) father's sister

gaam – (Gujerati) village in India

ghee – (Gujerati) clarified butter

gulab jamun – (Hindi) an Indian sweet consisting of a ball of deep-fried paneer boiled in a sugar syrup

hadith – (Arabic) reports, statements or actions of the Prophet Muhammad (PBUH)

Hadrat – (Arabic) title used to honour a person

halaal – (Arabic) term designating an action or object as permissible according to Islamic law

halaqat – (Arabic) religious gathering

haleem – (Arabic) stew composed of meat, lentils and wheat that has been pounded into a thick paste

hifz – (Arabic) committing the Quran to memory

hijab – (Arabic) any head, face, or body covering worn by Muslim women or men that conforms to a standard of modesty

hijabista – (Arabic slang) a Muslim woman or girl who dresses stylishly while conforming to the Islamic modesty code (hijab)

hikmah – (Arabic) wisdom

iddat – (Arabic) period of waiting that a woman must observe after the death of her spouse or a divorce, during which she may not marry another man; its purpose is to ensure that the male parent of any offspring produced after the cessation of a nikah (marriage) would be known

iftaar – (Arabic) the meal eaten by Muslims after sunset during Ramadan

imaan – faith

Imam – (Arabic) person holding an Islamic leadership position; often the worship leader of a mosque and Muslim community

indaba – (isiZulu and isiXhosa) problem or concern

Insha'Allah – (Arabic) God willing

istikhara – (Arabic) prayer performed in order to receive divine guidance from Allah

izzat – (Arabic) respect

jadoo – (Persian) magic

jamaat – (Arabic) an Islamic council or assembly

jamiat – (Arabic) a term that, in an Islamic context, refers to a political party or other organisation

jee – (Urdu) yes

jungli – (Hindi) uncultured, wild

kachumber – (Hindi) a salad of chopped onion, tomato, cucumber, and sometimes other vegetables, typically seasoned with chilli and coriander, served as an accompaniment to a main meal

khala or khalama – (Gujerati) mother's sister

kheema-kow – (Hindi) mince rice dish

khowse – Burmese coconut-based soup served with spaghetti/noodles and sides of onions, and coriander

khul – annulment of marriage upon the wife returning the mahr

khuri – (Hindi) a saucy mixture of sour milk, green chillies, salt and other spices

khuri kitchri – (Hindi) yellow rice dish with an assortment of side dishes

kurta – (Persian) loosely fitting, long shirt worn by males

laddoo – (Hindi) Indian sweet made from a mixture of flour, sugar, and shortening shaped into a ball

madressah – (Arabic) institution for acquiring Islamic knowledge

mahr – (Arabic) dowry paid to the wife upon marriage

mamajee – (Gujerati) mother's brother

masala – (Urdu) mixture of spices used for cooking

mashwara – (Arabic) consultation

mashwera – (Arabic) mutual consultation

masi – (Gujerati) mother's sister

masjid – (Arabic) mosque/place of worship for followers of Islam

Memon – people who originate from a region in North, India

mendhi – (Hindi) dye used to make patterns on a girl's or woman's hand; also commonly known as henna

mithai – (Hindi) sweet meats

Moulana – (Arabic) title given to Muslim religious leaders and graduates of religious institutions

musallah – (Arabic) prayer mat

Muslimah – (Arabic) a Muslim woman

naana – (Gujerati) maternal grandfather

naani – (Gujerati) maternal grandmother

nafl – (Arabic) optional Muslim salaah (formal worship)

nazar – (Arabic) look or stare to bring evil or misfortune

nikah – (Arabic) Muslim marriage contract

niqab – (Arabic) a veil worn by some Muslim women in public, covering all of the face apart from the eyes

PBUH – abbreviation for 'Peace be upon him'

puri patha – (Gujerati) is a fried flat bread best served with Patha (madumbi leaves rolled with a spicy gram flour paste)

Quran – the Muslim holy book

qurbani – (Arabic) practice of sacrificing an animal, such as a sheep, goat or camel on the day of Eid-ul-Adha, in order to remember the willingness of Ebrahim to sacrifice his son Ismail as an act of his obedience to the Allah

Ramadaan – (Arabic) ninth month of the Muslim calendar, during which Muslims observe fasting

rizq – (Arabic) provision

roti – (Gujerati) bread made from stoneground wholemeal flour

sabr – (Arabic) patience or endurance

sadaqah – (Arabic) charity

salaah – (Arabic) practice of formal worship in Islam

samoosa – (Persian) baked or fried triangular-shaped savory

seerah – (Arabic) from a verb that means 'to travel'; the biography of a person is called 'seerah' because when we read it, we are essentially travelling the person's journey

Sharíah – Islamic law based on the teachings of the Quran and the traditions of the Prophet Muhammad (PBUH)

sheikh – (Arabic) Islamic scholar who is awarded the title after graduation

shukr – (Arabic) thank you

sojee – (Hindi) semolina

suhoor – (Arabic) a meal eaten before sunrise by Muslims during Ramadan

sujood – prostration to Allah in the direction of the Kaaba at Mecca, which is usually done during the daily salaah (formal worship)

sunnah – (Arabic) any action that was said, done or liked by the holy prophet Muhammad (PBUH)

surah – (Arabic) chapter in the holy Quran

taalim – (Arabic) Islamic educational programme

tafseer – (Arabic) critical explanation or interpretation of the Quran

tahaarah – (Arabic) purification

talaq – divorce

taqdeer – (Arabic) doctrine of fate or pre-destination

tarkari – (Gujerati) spicy curry

udhaar – (Urdu) on loan

ulema – (Arabic) body of Muslim scholars recognised as having specialist knowledge of Islamic sacred law and theology

ummah – (Arabic) nation or community

Umrah – pilgrimage made to the holy lands of Makkah, which can take place any time of the year, except during the Hajj period

vagaar – (Gujerati) fried onions used in Indian cuisine

velan – (Gujerati) thin, wooden rolling pin

vrou – (Afrikaans) wife

wudhu – (Arabic) ablution

zina – (Arabic) adultery, fornication

www.ingramcontent.com/pod-product-compliance
Lightning Source LLC
Chambersburg PA
CBHW020110010526
44115CB00008B/777